AIDING THE

MALADJUSTED PUPIL

AIDING THE MALADJUSTED PUPIL

A GUIDE

FOR TEACHERS

by R. MURRAY THOMAS

University of California, Santa Barbara

DAVID McKAY COMPANY, INC.

NEW YORK

AIDING THE MALADJUSTED PUPIL

LIBRARY OF CONGRESS CATALOG CARD NUMBER: 67-10984
MANUFACTURED IN THE UNITED STATES OF AMERICA

To
Minnabeth T. Garrison
and
Elinor T. Guinn

CONTENTS

CONTENTS

Preface

This volume offers what the writer believes most teachers need as they attempt to aid children and youth solve personal-social adjustment problems:

1. A noncomplex personality theory that can improve an instructor's ability to diagnose pupils' social-psychological difficulties.

2. An analysis of the teacher's role and the clinician's role in aiding disturbed students so that teachers may determine the proper limits of their responsibilities for solving maladjusted students' problems.

3. A description of the principal ways that teachers, within their daily instructional routine, can identify those students who need aid and can gain insight into the bases for the disturbed students' problems.

4. A series of case studies to illustrate in specific classroom terms the ways that teachers and therapists have diagnosed a variety of personal-social difficulties at different age levels. And equally important, the studies need to show what attempts teachers have made to help the students and how well the attempts succeeded.

In compiling the case studies that compose the final four chapters, the writer was aided by the following teachers and psychologists who described approaches they had used in working with maladjusted children and youth: Harland D. Bentley, Jean Crist, Kathleen Crotty, Jack Jones, Wilmuth R. McBeth, Saylor S. Milton, Dorothy Morris, Dennis Naiman, Donald Skipworth, Frederick G. Smith, Margaret Smith, Mary Stringer, Lois Van Schaick, Eugene J. Ward, and Marion L. Whelpley. The writer gratefully acknowledges their contributions, as well as the aid of the administrators of schools in Goleta, Santa Barbara, and Santa Paula, California, who provided sources of case material.

Part One

PERSONALITY THEORY FOR CLASSROOM USE

There is probably no more controversial area in psychology than that of personality assessment. Underlying the controversy is a more basic lack of agreement about the structure of personality and about the reasons one individual's personality is different from another's.

What this state of affairs means for the classroom teacher is that there are no completely sure answers to such questions as:

> When a pupil's behavior differs markedly from that of his classmates, how do I know whether he is emotionally disturbed and needs help or whether he is merely expressing a healthy individuality?
>
> Are acts of aggression symptoms of maladjustment?
>
> Is every shy child in need of help?
>
> Can a student appear to get along well with others, yet really be so emotionally disturbed that he needs aid?

These questions and scores of similar ones force themselves daily upon teachers who are concerned about the overall development of their students. Science has yet to provide us with perfect answers for them. But teachers cannot await the ultimate scientific solution before they act. They must treat students on the basis of the most reasonable theory of personality and the most convenient methods of assessment available to them now, imperfect as these may sometimes prove.

The purpose of Part One is to describe briefly a theory of personality structure, an approach to personality assessment, a cluster of generalizations about learning better methods of adjustment, and a discussion of ways the pupil's environment can be altered to suit his needs.

PERSONALITY THEORY
FOR CLASSROOM USE

There is probably no more complete agreement . . . along
than that of personality assessment. Trying this there never
is a more basic lack of agreement about the nature of
pursuit . . . and about the number . . . individuals personality
is different from another.

What this state of affairs means for the classroom teacher is
that there are no completely sure answers to such questions as:

When a pupil's behavior differs markedly from that of his
classmates, how do I know whether he is an average, disturbed and in need of help or whether he is merely expressing a
healthy individuality?

Are signs of depression symptoms of maladjustment?
Is anxiety a sign of ill in need of help?
Can a student appear to get along well with others, yet really
be emotionally disturbed that I . . . his aid?

These questions and others of similar nature . . . themselves
daily upon teachers who are concerned about the intellectual development of their students . . . don't know to prepare us with verified
answers for them. Researchers cannot state the blunter . . . the
solution is there a . . . correct. This must treat students on the basis
of the most reasonable theory of personality and the most consistent method or present that available to them now. In practice
this is not done in a purposeful way.

The purpose of . . . following chapters . . . those of us as
only a scholarly approach to . . . consider how merely a start
. . . thinking . . . about . . . and exert attitude of experiment.
The education of ways the pupil's individual can be created
to satisfying needs.

CHAPTER 1

A VIEW OF
PERSONALITY STRUCTURE

A basic question that teachers often ask may serve as the starting point of our discussion: What is good mental health or good personal-social adjustment?

Although various psychologists, philosophers, religious workers, and laymen may answer this query in somewhat different ways, one definition that many of them agree upon is:

> The psychologically well-adjusted person (1) fulfills all of his own needs without postponing any of them too long and (2) does not interfere unduly with other people fulfilling their needs; indeed, he helps them meet their needs.

This definition places a dual commitment on the individual: a responsibility to himself (the personal aspect) and a responsibility to others (the social aspect). Or, viewed another way, the individual constantly has two kinds of demands exerted on him: those of his internal needs and those of his environment. The decision-making aspect of personality is charged with finding the best techniques to satisfy these two agencies whose demands are frequently not very compatible. These three factors may be charted as follows:

INTERNAL NEEDS	EGO or SELF	ENVIRONMENT
Demand immediate $\longrightarrow$ satisfaction.	Makes decisions to satisfy both needs and environment as well as possible.	$\longleftarrow$ (PHYSICAL and SOCIAL) Provides opportunities and makes demands.

If we may risk personification for a moment, we can say that the need-system is demanding: "I want fulfillment immediately

3

and completely for all my desires, regardless of all else." So the need-system (labeled the *id* by Freud) is selfish and asocial. The environment states: "Here are the opportunities for satisfying your needs; but note carefully the restrictions, the rules, society's customs, and the responsibilities. If you do not play within the rules, you are punished by the withholding of things that you desire." The ego or self, caught between these two demands, constantly grapples with life's great problem: How can I best fulfill all the needs as immediately as possible and still meet the demands of the environment?

To make the nature of these three components of personality clearer, we shall inspect each more closely.

KINDS OF NEEDS

No one has ever seen a need as such. Needs are merely constructs we have created to explain the probable motives behind people's actions. For instance, we experience stomach contractions, fatigue, and vague states of discomfort which we are accustomed to calling *hunger* or *appetite*. When these conditions arise, we find ourselves seeking certain substances to chew and swallow so our discomfort will disappear and we will experience pleasure and well-being. Man has labeled the supposed cause behind these particular periodic discomforts *the food need*. Like the food need, any other need is a lack which the organism strives to fulfill. Some unfulfilled need or lack underlies each of our waking or sleeping thoughts and acts. When we view such a lack as being the force which pushes us to think and act, it is called a *drive,* in this case the *hunger drive*.

In addition to the food need, what are the others that man constantly is striving to satisfy? Scientists and philosophers who have attempted to answer this question have agreed in general on the rather apparent physiological ones like the needs for oxygen, drink, moderate environmental temperature, the avoidance of harm to the body, and the expulsion of waste products. There is also widespread agreement on a need for sexual expression, though the ways this can properly be satisfied are not agreed upon.

But since many of our daily acts are apparently not directed toward satisfying a physiological lack, it is appropriate to postulate also the existence of social-psychological needs. These have been difficult to label and define because one particular act is not necessarily directed toward meeting a particular need, as eating and drinking and breathing tend to be. Apparently a diversity of acts may be used by different people to satisfy the same need. For instance, a striving for *social recognition* is satisfied by one man through his owning an expensive automobile, by another man through being elected president of a luncheon club, and by a third through writing a novel. Further difficulty encountered in delineating and labeling social-psychological needs is caused by the fact that the same act—such as going to a school dance—may be used by different people to fulfill different needs. One girl may attend the dance in search of affection, another for social recognition, a third to experience a feeling of self-worth because dancing is the thing she does best, and a fourth for the sake of curiosity because she has never before been to a dance.

Though the exact nature and names of all social-psychological needs have not been agreed upon, we can cite a number of them whose identity is rather widely accepted, such as: (1) a desire for approval from others, (2) a desire for recognition, (3) a need for affection, (4) curiosity, (5) a need for a feeling of accomplishment, (6) a striving for self-respect, and (7) a drive for mastery over the environment.

Some psychologists recognize individual needs like those of hunger and affection, but they believe these are merely subneeds that are subservient to one all-encompassing need which serves as the organizing mainspring of life. This all-inclusive human need has been identified by a variety of labels, like the need for self-sufficiency, for self-adequacy, for the maintenance and enhancement of the personality, or for the organization and control of one's fate. Combs and Snygg, who have espoused this point of view, argue their case in these terms:

Man lives in a changing world, a world in which the organizations of which he is composed and of which he is part are continuously changing. A changing world requires changes in the organization of the self if it is to be maintained. Each of us needs to do more than merely change with the flow of events. Because we are aware of the future and must maintain ourselves, in the future as well as in the present, it is necessary to enhance the self against the exigencies of tomorrow. The self, therefore, has to be maintained in the future, built up and enhanced so that the individual feels secure for tomorrow. And since the future is uncertain and unknown, no enhancement of the individual's experience of personal value, no degree of self-actualization, is ever enough. Human beings are, by nature, insatiable. . . . Whenever we refer to man's basic need, we mean that *great driving, striving force in each of us by which we are continually seeking to make ourselves ever more adequate to cope with life.*[1]

Some psychologists believe that social-psychological or self-enhancement needs or motives are not inborn but are learned and have their foundation in the more basic physiological ones. This issue of the origin of needs, however, is not of much practical importance to the typical teacher. For him the important thing is that social-psychological needs exist in school-age children and youth and these needs motivate most of the pupils' thoughts and acts.

From the viewpoint of individual differences, we can note that some of the variations in personality found in a given classroom will be caused at least partly by differences in the strength of various pupils' needs. Whereas all of the students apparently have the same basic needs which tend to make for similarity in their feelings and acts, the fact that these needs arise in different strengths and at different times tends to make pupils different from one another. A pupil with a low energy level will require more rest than one with much vitality, and their behavior in school will reflect these differences. The sixth-grade girl whose glandular development causes her to reach puberty early will probably display different sexual drives and greater heterosexual interest than her slower maturing classmates.

[1] Arthur W. Combs and Donald Snygg. *Individual Behavior*. New York: Harper & Row, Inc., 1959, pp. 45–46. Reprinted by permission.

THE ENVIRONMENT'S OPPORTUNITIES
AND DEMANDS

In the main, the human organism cannot fulfill its needs within itself. It is true that a desire for recognition or for feelings of accomplishment may be satisfied to some degree through fantasy or dreams. And certain varieties of mental illness cause the individual to escape from reality into a make-believe world in which the social-psychological desires are met. But every individual must traffic with his environment to meet almost all physiological needs, and for most people the satisfaction of social-psychological needs also demands transactions outside of their own minds and bodies.

Just as people have basic needs in common—a fact that urges them toward similarity in thought and action—so they also share some common environmental influences which mold a degree of sameness into their personalities. Within a typical classroom, some of the common elements are language, school lessons, governmental and school laws and rules, generally accepted customs in the society, climate and weather, scenes and objects viewed each day, and similarities in parental customs, television viewing habits, and the like. On the other hand, there are always environmental factors unique to each child and youth which impel the personality toward uniqueness. The oldest child in the family has a different environment than the youngest, the child of a bitter and crippled father is influenced toward developing a personality different from that of a child with a vigorous and attentive one, and the youth whose whining mother tries to bind him to her psychologically is affected differently than the youth who has no mother.

In growing up socially, the child is like a visitor to a foreign land who is introduced to the customs of the country by guides or agents. For most children the most important guides are their parents. Other agents who also influence a child's understanding of the new land are his brothers and sisters, teachers, playmates, and such mass communication media as television and comic books. These all interpret for him the demands and opportunities

of his society. The typical child's day is flooded with adult interpretations, instructions, and admonitions:

> If you shovel food into your mouth like that, people will
> think you're some kind of animal.
>
> Don't you dare use the word *damn* again.
>
> I don't want you to pick a fight; but if somebody else starts
> one, don't you run away from it.
>
> Girls your age don't climb trees.
>
> If you speak that way to the other children, none of them
> will like you.
>
> What a clean, beautiful girl we have, and how nice you've
> kept your dress.
>
> I'll give you a quarter for every A on your report card.
>
> If you don't do your homework, you'll flunk, and there'll be
> no college for you.

To ensure that the very young child abides by these standards
of behavior, adults must use physical force or some other clear
form of punishment and reward like withholding affection or
privileges. This is because the child is not naturally obedient. The
environment must directly enforce its demands. But as the child
grows older, we observe that the adults' earlier admonishing and
complimenting, warning and wheedling, threatening and rewarding have made permanent marks on his personality. He gradually
has incorporated parents' and teachers' and peers' standards of
behavior into his own personality. No longer is it necessary for
the adult always to be on hand to make sure the child complies.
The older child now often abides by the standards himself.
Although he still operates on the basis of punishment and reward,
he himself is now the policing agent. His own personality rewards him with pride when he lives up to society's standards and
punishes him with guilt when he violates them.

This internal representative of the environment that gradually
develops as the child matures has been labeled the *superego*.
Like a coin, it displays two faces. One, called the *ego ideal*, con-
tains the individual's conception of the kinds of traits and behavior that are admirable, proper, and noble. When he thinks

and acts in keeping with these standards of goodness, he experiences the pleasures of pride and self-respect. The other face is the *conscience*. It represents the individual's ideas of what is sinful, wrong, unfair, improper, and despicable. When he acts in any of these sinful or improper ways, his conscience punishes him with guilt, shame, and self-contempt.

At this point it is desirable for us to revise our earlier diagram of the components of personality to include this internalized representative of the environment, the superego.

PHYSIOLOGICAL and SOCIAL-PSYCHOLOGICAL NEEDS Demand immediate satisfaction.	*EGO or SELF* Makes decisions ⟶ to satisfy needs, superego, and environment as well as possible.	*ENVIRONMENT* (PHYSICAL and SOCIAL) ⟵ Provides opportunities and makes demands.

SUPEREGO
(INTERNAL REPRESENTATIVE
of STANDARDS)
Demands conformance to
standards by rewarding
with pride, punishing
with guilt and shame.

When we accept the proposition that a person's ideas of right and wrong are not inborn but are learned from his particular environment, we recognize that no two people will have precisely the same ego ideal and conscience. It should then come as no surprise that one boy will experience little or no guilt when he steals from the teacher's purse, whereas another boy will feel sharp pangs of conscience simply at the thought of this act. Similarly, a high-school girl whose parents rather openly engage in extramarital sexual relations may feel no shame at having frequent intercourse with various boys, whereas another girl who has received strong, dire warnings from her parents about relations with boys may cringe with shame at letting a boy kiss her good-night.

Teachers who fail to recognize the fact that all consciences are not identical are apt to make frequent errors when they try to understand student behavior and try to influence it. The treatment that effectively guides one pupil's actions may be unsuitable for another whose feelings of pride and guilt are seated in a different set of internal standards.

In sum, the child daily interacts with his environment as he strives to fulfill his needs. Gradually, as he matures, he internalizes standards and values that his society urges upon him. These standards become an intimate, inescapable facet of his personality, influencing his thoughts and acts by rewarding him with pride and punishing him with guilt and shame.

THE EGO OR SELF, ARBITER OF INTERNAL AND EXTERNAL DEMANDS

As noted earlier, the ego (self) or decision-making aspect of the personality is the recipient of the demands of the needs, of the environment, and—as the child matures—of the superego. The ego is the problem solver that must develop techniques to satisfy diverse needs in light of the environment's opportunities and rules and in keeping with an ego ideal and conscience. These techniques have been labeled *ego-adjustment mechanisms* or *ego-defense mechanisms*. They compose all of our daily acts. Each thing we do every moment of our lives, waking or sleeping, is directed toward maximum need satisfaction within the limits set by the environment and superego.

From the standpoint of understanding individual differences in personality, there are two aspects of the ego's operation that are of particular importance to teachers. These are: (1) the individualized way the ego interprets reality and (2) the nature and patterning of a person's adjustment mechanisms.

INDIVIDUALIZED PERCEPTION OF REALITY

When a first-grade girl entered the classroom one morning with a four-foot-long snake in a jar, several children screamed and ran to the rear of the room, several more watched cautiously from a short distance, but three boys stepped forward and peered closely at the animal. One of them announced, "It's a king snake. Here, let me hold it." He unscrewed the jar lid, lifted the snake out gently, and draped it around his neck.

This incident illustrates the commonly observed fact that one person often reacts differently to the same object or event than does another person. The basic reason they react differently is that the event has a different meaning for each of them. And the reason it has a different meaning is that the perceiving or interpreting aspect of their minds is not the same in each case. For instance, the children who ran screaming saw the snake as meaning an undesirable object that strangles and bites venomously. The children who kept a cautious distance had perhaps learned that some snakes are harmful and some are harmless, but they could not distinguish which kind this was. The boy who lifted the snake from the jar had learned to distinguish poisonous from nonpoisonous ones, and he recognized the snake's yellow and black stripes as signifying a harmless king snake—a kind he had handled before without injury.

In the field of psychology a variety of terms have been used to refer to this aspect of the ego that predisposes one person to interpret events and objects differently than does another. One expression in long use is *apperceptive mass*. This designates the mass of memories and the pressure of current needs which serve as the lens through which new events and objects are interpreted. The pupil never receives new information into a fresh, unmarked mind. Instead, each new event's meaning is colored by his memories of similar past events and by the current state of his needs-system.

The expression *apperceptive mass* has been used for more than a hundred years to describe a person's individualized view of life, but in recent decades other terms meaning substantially the same thing have been coined. *Life space* and *phenomenological self* are two such terms. When we use the concept implied by these terms—that a person's actions are best understood if we know his unique perception of the world and of himself—we are said to be using a *perceptual* or *personal* or *phenomenological* approach to interpreting human behavior.

The apperceptive mass is a kind of mental map. An individual's mental map is supposed to represent a complex territory that includes the physical world, the attitudes of other people toward him, the desirability of other people, the rules of society, his own needs, his own abilities, demands of his conscience, and the like. Most people are constantly revising these charts as new experiences suggest that corrections are in order. Some people, accused of having "closed minds," resist altering a satisfying map despite new information they receive about the territory—that is, new information about "reality." People whose mental charts are markedly out of order often turn to psychiatrists, clinical psychologists, and ministers for help in correcting the inaccuracies.

There are several reasons that one person's apperceptive mass or view of life differs from another's. First, two individuals may at the same moment be experiencing *different needs*. The man who has just alighted carsick after a fast ride down a twisting mountain road will interpret the sight of a shrimp-and-oyster cocktail differently than will a famished gourmet who has unwillingly fasted all day. Second, the condition of a person's *sense organs* affects his perception. An individual who is hard of hearing operates within a different world of impressions than one with acute hearing. A person under the influence of marijuana or LSD perceives himself and others differently than a person not affected by drugs. Third, the differences between two people's *intelligence* (ability to recognize relationships between past experiences and various new stimuli) will modify the meaning a new event or object will have for them. When a quantity of water splashes into the canoe, one girl inefficiently begins to scoop it out with her cupped palm, whereas her companion sees her sailor cap as a potentially efficient bucket.

Fourth, and perhaps most important, one person's *experiences* have taught him to expect different consequences from events and objects than have another person's. A girl whose mother has shielded her from every potential physical injury by cautioning, "Don't try that—you'll get hurt," will interpret opportunities for new adventures differently than will the child whose mother has usually said, "Try it yourself, and I'll be here to help if you need it."

It seems clear that the teacher who best understands the student's unique mental map is the one in the best position to analyze the student's behavior and, if it is undesirable behavior, to alter it. Ways of gaining this understanding are discussed in Chapter 6.

PATTERNS OF ADJUSTMENT MECHANISMS

The newborn child's mechanisms for dealing with the environment and for fulfilling his needs are very meager. They consist mostly of crying and flailing the arms and legs. But the nervous system and control over the muscles develop rapidly so that the infant soon expands his skills. Instead of simply whining when he is hungry, he grasps the nearby bottle and puts it to his mouth. He rolls over to relieve the pinch of the toy he has lain upon. He discovers that of all the noises he makes, the one that brings the most prompt and willing attention is "ma-ma." The young child's life consists of experiences which strengthen old methods of satisfying needs or which cause him to learn new, more adequate ones. Hence, by the time he enters school his repertoire of ego-adjustment mechanisms is usually quite broad. The school years produce ever-expanding, more sophisticated additions to this repertoire.

For convenience in discussing techniques of adjustment, psychologists have categorized the mechanisms and have applied such names and definitions as the following:

Direct Action means any behavior, mental or physical, which straightforwardly satisfies a need. The hungry boy uses this as he makes and consumes a peanut-butter sandwich. The teen-age girl uses it when, yearning for affection, she telephones her boyfriend and invites him to take her for an evening walk.

Is direct action a desirable adjustment mechanism? The answer depends upon how it functions in the particular individual's life. It is desirable when it provides immediate release from the tension of an unsatisfied need and when at the same time it is suited to the environment's rules or demands. But sometimes direct action is either impossible or unwise. The hungry boy who is stranded in the desert without food will find direct action impossible. The teen-age girl who tries to gain affection by accosting young men on the street may find her tactic unwise if it results in her being arrested or labeled with a reputation that causes her friends to shun her.

Compensation is the emphasis of one kind of behavior in order to overcome some personal or environmental barrier.

One form of this mechanism is *direct compensation,* which means that the individual tries to strengthen himself in an area in which he feels inferior. For instance, an undersized junior-high-school boy may spend most of his spare time in body-building exercises. A high-school girl whose academic abilities fall short of her scholarly ambitions may compensate by spending extra hours on homework and by not permitting herself to view any television programs other than ones about serious scientific or social issues.

Direct compensation is often a proper ego technique, for it requires the individual to admit of a real weakness and to make a straightforward attempt to overcome the weakness. But direct compensation can be a frustrating, maladjustive mechanism if the individual persists in using it in the face of sure defeat. If the short son of short ancestors dedicates all of his spare time to stretching exercises which he hopes will make him a six-footer, he not only is doomed to defeat by genetics but his exercising also wastes many hours which could profitably be used for satisfying other needs and for meeting his responsibilities.

A second form of this mechanism is *indirect* or *displaced* compensation. The individual who suffers a weakness tries to make up for it by substituting attainments in some other area of life. The short boy may become a flyweight wrestler rather than trying to stretch himself to a proper height for basketball. The girl with few academic talents may concentrate on personal appearance or on cooking and sewing skills that will enhance her attractiveness as a potential wife. Indirect compensation is often a most desirable form of adjustment. But it is inappropriate if it causes the individual to neglect an important weakness which he could and should strengthen directly rather than circumvent. This device is also unsuitable if the substitute act or skill fails to satisfy the particular need that has been frustrated.

Identification means the extension of the self or ego to include other people or objects from the environment. That is, the person embraces within his own self-concept the characteristics and welfare of individuals, groups, and objects beyond himself. This mechanism serves two important functions:

First, it motivates a person to mold himself in the form of an idealized acquaintance or group or idea. The young boy who admires his father's abilities and knowledge and power thus identifies with his father and strives to pattern his own behavior and appearance after this ideal. Therefore, identification accounts for much of the similar behavior we find among people within the same family or social group.

Second, identification furnishes vicarious need fulfillment. The successes and failures of the idealized model are experienced by the child as being his own successes and failures. When the movie star receives an Academy Award, the adolescent girl who identifies with the star glows with pride. When the young boy's father is bested by a rival in golf, the boy is depressed.

Identification is a desirable mechanism when it causes a young person to design his behavior in the image of a proper ideal, of someone whose behavior is admirable. It is also valuable for expanding pupils' understanding of the world and for furnishing them through books and television the dangerous experiences and satisfactions which they could not obtain directly. But identification becomes maladjustive if the child fashions his life after the model of people whose traits will lead him into subsequent difficulties, as is often true when he idealizes gangsters or people whose distorted and punitive consciences cause them to enter pseudoreligious movements. Furthermore, identification is undesirable if it causes the individual to limit his satisfactions to vicarious ones with the result that he never faces his own problems realistically in order to solve them directly.

Physical or Psychological Escape means running away from difficulties. The retreat is physical when it involves running from an angry dog or leaving the room in the midst of an argument. It is psychological escape when it involves mentally moving away from the conflict or the frustrating situation, as in the case of the sixth-grade girl who withdraws from a page of arithmetic problems by daydreaming about owning a horse which she will ride in parades. People who tire of creating their own fantasies are aided by television, motion pictures, and paperback books which furnish an endless supply of escape routes.

Both physical and psychological withdrawal are beneficial when they enable the individual to save himself from difficulties which he could never solve or which he could not solve at the moment. The school boy who is attacked by a gang is probably wise to outrun them rather than plead for mercy or take a beating. The business executive whose responsibilities have reduced him to a harried insomniac may well benefit from a three-week vacation at a mountain retreat. The girl who still is dependent upon her parents for financial support may adjust to her mother's continual nagging by mentally shutting out the sound, and at the same time indulging in pleasant fantasies of her own.

However, escape is undesirable when overused. It can prevent the individual from facing many problems which he could, if he tried, conquer directly so he never need fear them again. It can cause him to neglect his responsibilities to other people and thus to suffer guilt and shame. In an extreme form, psychological escape is symptomatic of psychosis, and the sufferer will require psychiatric care. The most irreversible form of escape is suicide.

One of the most perplexing questions facing the teacher is: To what extent do a given pupil's thoughts simply represent psychological escape and to what extent do they represent creative thinking? For instance, a boy may be reading *Robin Hood,* but for which of these motives: to escape his responsibility to learn a list of spelling words, to gain vicarious satisfactions in the area of physical deeds because he is unwilling to compete in football with his agemates, to learn the causes and political-social atmosphere that led to the Magna Charta, to analyze the plot and dialogue of the tale so he can write his own adventure stories, or to accomplish all of these? During a grammar lesson the high-school girl who daydreams about a career as a television actress may only be escaping the grammar task, or she may actually be forming realistic plans for improving her appearance and her acting skills so as to attain her goal.

Rationalization is a form of self-deception or an attempt to deceive others.

One subtype of rationalization is called *sour grapes,* a label derived from the fable of the fox who could not reach the high grapevine, so he pronounced the fruit sour, thus blaming the environment rather than himself for his lack of success. The child who receives a low test mark and then declares, "That stupid teacher never could make up a fair test," is using the fox's adjustment technique.

A second subtype has been labeled *sweet lemon* in reference to the person who mistakenly chooses a bitter fruit but does not wish the onlookers to notice his foolish error, so he claims, "This lemon is quite sweet—just what I wanted." Little Orphan Annie and Pollyanna habitually use this mechanism. This form of adjustment can be desirable. By perceiving some good in unfortunate events the person suffering the misfortune is consoled and thus may find the strength or optimism to carry on. But when sweet-lemon rationalization is used habitually it may alienate the individual's companions who come to regard this trait as a mark of insincerity, as in the case of the high-school boy who declares: "It's a good thing I wasn't elected president of the class, because the job takes up so much time I wouldn't be able to get my studying done."

A third form of rationalization has been called the *doctrine of balances* because the person who uses it seems to believe that for every liability in one's life there is a counterbalancing asset, and vice versa. This doctrine is reflected in such maxims as "beautiful but dumb," "smart but frail," and "blessed are the meek for they shall inherit the earth." Although such a habit of thinking is useful for bringing solace to the unbeautiful, the unsmart, and the meek, its scientific validity in the cases of these three maxims is apparently nonexistent.

The main virtue of rationalization as an adjustment device lies in the temporary protection it offers the individual from loss of self-respect or loss of reputation when he has been thwarted. His rationalization may permit him to allay discouragement until he has been able to regain his psychological equilibrium and face the real problem squarely. But if he habitually rationalizes and thus always fails to admit his own shortcomings or to improve them, he may expect serious psychological maladjustment.

Repression is the process of unwittingly pushing problems out of consciousness and into the unconscious mind. The person who represses is not knowingly burying his troubles. Rather, his ego in an unconscious act pushes difficulties from consciousness in order to relieve him of problems which he does not seem able to solve in any other way.

Repression is desirable when it clears the conscious mind of minor concerns which would distract the individual from concentrating on daily tasks. But it is undesirable when the repressed material consists of major problems and unfulfilled needs which thereafter seethe unsolved in the unconscious and precipitate such symptoms as unreasonable anxieties, fears, anger, guilt, tremors, headaches, ulcers, compulsive acts, obsessive thoughts, and the like.

Negativism is a refusal to do what is asked or required. For example, when the kindergarten teacher asks a boy to allow a girl her turn on the rocking horse, the boy silently shows he rejects the request as he locks his arms and legs tightly around the horse's body. There are occasions when negativism is an appropriate adjustment mechanism, such as when a girl stubbornly refuses to carry out delinquent acts urged upon her by older students. However, frequent refusals to carry out requests and responsibilities of a reasonable nature are marks of maladjustment.

Aggression means striking out at some person or object, either physically or verbally. Aggression is labeled *direct* when it is aimed at the person or agency which the individual believes has frustrated his attempts to satisfy his needs. A girl is directly aggressive when she pulls the hair of a classmate who has teased her. A teacher is using direct aggression when he attacks a wayward student with sarcasm.

Aggression is termed *indirect* or *displaced* when it is vented against a person or object other than the one which has frustrated the individual. The boy who is criticized by the teacher for doing poorly in arithmetic may then behave contritely before the teacher but later write vulgar phrases on the lavatory wall. The girl whose mother nags her about being overweight does not answer back; instead, she criticizes the nicely shaped girls in her class at school.

Direct aggression is often an appropriate mechanism when it serves to protect the individual from people who attempt to violate his rights. However, when either direct or indirect aggression is used to exploit others or when it becomes the dominating style of life adjustment, it is undesirable. For some children and youth, this adjustment device is particularly damaging because an emotionally charged burst of aggression causes them subsequent feelings of strong guilt. In short, they suffer the double censure of environment and conscience.

Regression means handling frustration by adopting kinds of behavior that were used at an earlier stage of life but which have later been relinquished in favor of more mature behavior. This is the device tried by a high-school girl who screams, throws herself on the bed, and thrashes her arms and legs after her mother has refused to let her buy a new record player. Regression has some positive value in that it affords the individual a release from the emotional tension which frustrations have caused. It also sometimes enables the person to obtain his immediate demand because the "childish" act embarrasses or intimidates the person who is frustrating him, like the young lady who breaks into tears to force a gentleman to grant her wishes. But more often regression is an inadequate method of solving problems, for it is disapproved by society and may prevent the individual from developing more mature ways of adjustment.

The foregoing list of ego-adjustment techniques does not pretend to represent a complete cataloguing of all mechanisms people use. Instead, the purpose of the list has been: (1) to illustrate the basic nature of several of the most prominent mechanisms and (2) to point out that a given mechanism cannot in itself be labeled good or bad. Rather, the goodness or badness of the technique is determined by the role it plays in the individual's life. Therefore, we cannot conclude that a child is maladjusted simply because he uses rationalization and repression. What is important to know is the extent to which he uses these mechanisms and the manner in which they fit into the pattern of his life.

Summary

This initial chapter has proposed a view of human personality which serves as a guide to analyzing the adequacy of a pupil's personal-social adjustment. This theory pictures all thought and action as being directed toward fulfilling needs within the limitations, and according to the opportunities, provided by the environment. The *ego* is proposed as being the decision-making function of the mind. The ego's task consists of assessing the inner needs and the environment, and then choosing the best action for satisfying the needs, the environment, and the internalized representative of the environment's standards (the superego). The techniques that the ego develops for satisfying these demands have been termed *adjustment mechanisms*.

CHAPTER 2

DEGREES OF PERSONAL-SOCIAL ADJUSTMENT

Utilizing the theory of personality outlined in Chapter 1, we can identify several different varieties of difficulties a person may suffer.

First, he may experience a conflict *between two or more needs.* A simple example of this would be that of a youth who returns to camp during a hunting trip and is so sleepy and hungry that he is perplexed about whether to eat first and then sleep or to sleep first and then eat. In the realm of psychological needs, an academically apt high-school girl may be disturbed by the conflict between her desire to date boys frequently, in order to fulfill needs for affection, and her desire to stay home most evenings to study, so as to become valedictorian of her graduating class and thus fulfill needs for high status in the eyes of parents, peers, and teachers.

Second, the conflict may arise *between inner needs and the superego.* This is a very common source of psychological difficulties. An academically inept child who never succeeds as well as his more able classmates will experience constant frustration in school work if his parents have built into him an ego ideal that demands, "You can do anything well if you only try hard enough." Likewise, an adolescent boy who experiences normal sexual drives can look forward to worry and guilt if he has developed a conscience that tells him, "Sex ideas and acts are sinful. They lead to insanity and to eternal damnation." In each of these examples, the individual has developed an inaccurate understanding of reality. His superego, as a proposed map of reality in the form of proper expectations, is inaccurately harsh. Just as an inaccurate map will lead to distressing errors and frustration on a journey, so an unduly harsh or lax understanding of life's standards can be expected to distress the child or youth.

21

Third, conflicts may arise between the individual's *needs and the environment*. A junior-high-school girl needs the self-respect and parental approval that will come from her entering the college-preparatory program in high school, but she is frustrated by her failure to master the algebra and French which are required for enrolling in the college-preparatory curriculum. Likewise, a girl who yearns for the independence to make her own decisions may continually be disturbed by her mother's making every decision for her.

In addition to these types of conflicts with the environment, there are others caused by the fact that the individual's concept of reality—other than the moral standards that form his superego—may be inaccurate. Thus he acts on the basis of certain assumptions about the world which are not true. This misjudgment causes psychological problems. A girl whose harsh father and domineering uncle have raised her to fear and suspect all males will tend to misjudge the gentle, thoughtful, and kindly men of the world unless her conception of reality is changed. Another variety of conflict, also based on a misconception of reality, results from an individual's using certain adjustment mechanisms for inappropriate situations. The child who successfully threw temper tantrums to fulfill needs when young will, as he grows older, conflict with many people who now expect more mature behavior from him. The person who has found fantasy to be a satisfying technique for avoiding problems will come into conflict with his society, which expects him to fulfill his responsibilities through direct action.

In summary, an individual may suffer at least two types of inner conflicts: a clash between incompatible needs or a clash between needs and conscience or ideals. In addition, he may suffer conflicts between his inner life and his environment. Some psychological problems involve a struggle among all of these elements of personality.

It is apparent that the foregoing types of conflicts can cause various degrees of maladjustment. A capable but careless student can experience a very minor clash between his need for respect and the environment on this occasion: he has just delivered an oral report to the class, and the teacher reacts to the presentation by criticizing the hasty, loose organization of the report. When criticized publicly, the boy feels embarrassed and angry at both the teacher and himself, but later he resolves to organize the next report more carefully. This incident has not disturbed his peace of mind for very long, nor has it interfered with his ability to pursue his normal life. We would conclude that this has been a common, normal, everyday incident which has brought temporary unpleasantness but, in the long run, has contributed in a positive way to the boy's ultimate adjustment.

Other students, however, face more serious problems. The parents of a high-school girl, in heated arguments during the past three months, have been threatening to divorce each other. Over this period of time the mother and father each have tried to win their daughter's exclusive affection and to alienate her from the other parent. The emotional trauma of this family conflict has weighed so heavily on the girl that she has suffered frequent headaches, has not been able to sleep well, and has not been able to concentrate on her studies. Before this open rift occurred between her parents, she apparently had led an efficient, happy life, socially as well as academically. If the current family conflict can be resolved, it is likely that she will again experience the normal adjustment she enjoyed earlier.

Although the high-school girl's disturbance may be temporary—the result of a recent conflict in her environment—some pupils' adjustment problems are chronic and deep-seated. A child who is very shy because he feels unworthy or because he finds the world unpredictable may, as a result of his shyness, constantly fail to have his needs for recognition, companionship, and affection satisfied. A youth who is chronically bellicose will continually be at odds with his society. A child whose home life has been unstable and whose parents have alternated between strict and indulgent treatment of him may show his desire for stability by being compulsively clean and neat. Other children may develop psychosomatic disorders, that is, physical symptoms like asthma or headaches that apparently have resulted from their repressing psychological conflicts which they could not solve consciously.

As the foregoing examples have suggested, psychological disturbances can be of varied degrees of seriousness. The degrees are perhaps best illustrated by the following scale which ranges from perfect adjustment at one end to extremely deviant behavior at the other.

Personal-Social Adjustment Scale

Perfect adjustment: all needs, all responsibilities satisfied.	*Normal adjustment:* some problems met and relatively well solved.	*Minor maladjustment:* disturbing problems in meeting needs and responsibilities.	*Neurotic adjustment:* chronic difficulties that upset life.	*Psychotic adjustment:* extremely disturbed behavior; inability to deal with life.

Earlier we defined the best possible adjustment as the simultaneous satisfaction of all needs and the fulfillment of all responsibilities or expectations of the environment. Clearly no one ever realizes such perfection, so no one deserves to be placed at the extreme left on this scale. Perhaps the best that a human can hope to accomplish is the sort of compromise labeled *normal adjustment:* some needs are not met promptly and some conflicts with the environment develop, but the individual generally manages to satisfy his most important wants most of the time within the limits his society imposes. So normal adjustment—meaning the type most people seem to achieve—is not free from problems and worries, but the problems which are met are typically solved without disrupting the individual's ability to face himself and his world. The boy in an earlier example who was criticized by an instructor for not organizing his oral report would fit into this normal-adjustment category.

A person usually does not maintain the same position on the adjustment scale throughout his life. From time to time he moves toward poorer or toward better adjustment. The girl whose parents were contemplating divorce exemplifies a student who was normally well adjusted until the divorce threat pressed her into the minor-maladjustment territory.

The term *neurosis* or *psychoneurosis* has been used by psychologists to encompass several kinds of personal-social maladjustments which cause the individual to be a frequent bother and worry to himself and/or to other people, but not a danger to himself or others. The term *neurotic* or *borderline-neurotic* might be applied to the kinds of children we described earlier as being chronically belligerent, compulsively clean and orderly, or ill without organic cause.

The most extreme personality disorders are labeled *psychoses*. People suffering from these disturbances are often a danger to themselves and/or to others, or else they are so poorly oriented to reality they cannot carry on their daily lives with any degree of efficiency. They may suffer from illusions, from fantasies which they believe to be real, from major states of depression or elation, or from delusions of grandeur or of persecution.

Most pupils will fall into the normal-adjustment category on the scale. They constantly meet minor frustrations, but they manage to marshal their psychological forces to solve their problems. In almost any classroom a small number of children are somewhat more disturbed, at least occasionally. They belong in the minor-maladjustment category. A still smaller percentage of students' disturbances are sufficiently chronic and bothersome to warrant the label neurotic or preneurotic. And only occasionally is there a student who sooner or later will experience a psychotic break. That is, his behavior will become so odd or threatening that he will require institutionalized treatment.

Summary

Students' maladjustments may result from conflicts between inner needs, from conflicts between needs and personal standards of conduct, from conflicts between needs and environmental opportunities or demands, or from an inaccurate concept of reality. These maladjustments may range in seriousness from routine daily problems that cause only a minor, passing disturbance to psychotic breakdowns which require that the individual be institutionalized. Any of these degrees of maladjustment may be observed among pupils in school.

CHAPTER 3

LEARNING BETTER ADJUSTMENT TECHNIQUES

As implied in the first two chapters, a maladjusted person may become better adjusted if:

1. He learns new ways to perceive life and new techniques for handling life's problems, or

2. His environment changes so it better fits the adjustment techniques he is accustomed to using, or

3. Both 1 and 2.

Chapter 3 focuses on the first of these: the process of revising the pupil's earlier, and now inappropriate, learnings. Chapter 4 focuses on ways of altering the pupil's environment so it better suits his abilities and his style of life.

WHAT LEARNINGS NEED REVISING?

Earlier we said that a person's concept of reality is like a map of a complex territory. If the map truly represents the landscape, each new path or barrier can be predicted and the traveler can decide to face or to avoid it. But if the map is inaccurate, the traveler will take wrong turns and will blunder into barriers. The task of the teacher or counselor, then, is to help pupils toward better adjustment by refining their mental maps to match more accurately the territory of the real world.

Or, to state the case in other terms, we can say that readjustment or therapy consists of helping the student revise his superego (ideals, concept of the rules of living) and/or his ego (the process of analyzing reality and of acting on the basis of this analysis) to fit the relation that exists between him and his environment.

Whether stated in terms of maps or of egos-superegos, the process is the same. It is a revision of past learnings to make his perceptions of life more accurate.

26

WHAT CAUSED THE INACCURATE PERCEPTIONS?

In trying to determine the reasons an individual holds a defective view of life, we may begin by asking: Why did he learn the wrong view in the first place? The answer is twofold: Either he received faulty information about the world or else he naïvely began interpreting new life situations from a viewpoint which he had learned under different conditions. So some people—because of bad information—actually have gained a defective original view. But others originally developed a viewpoint which was quite accurate for the conditions under which they were living at the time. Their trouble arose later when the environmental conditions changed but they failed to make the necessary alterations in their old perceptions. They tried to travel the new territory with an outmoded map.

We can illustrate the way these sources of inaccurate perceptions may develop if we inspect the cases of four maladjusted pupils.

Faulty Data from Faulty Receptors

In a first-grade classroom a series of the reactions of a girl named Helen at first puzzled the teacher. When the pupils were learning to tell time, Helen could accurately state the time on the drawings of clocks in the textbook but could not tell time from the clock on the wall. In arithmetic she worked problems correctly when she stood at the blackboard or worked from her book at her desk, but she could not suggest corrections for errors that classmates made on the blackboard. One afternoon when a helicopter flew low over the school during recess, Helen asked whether the plane had been carrying hundreds of passengers or just one or two. These incidents and other similar ones caused the teacher to ask the school nurse to test the girl's vision with a Snellen chart. The test confirmed the teacher's guess that Helen was seriously nearsighted, a fact that her parents had never realized.

As soon as Helen received glasses to correct her faulty vision, she discovered that she had to revise her learning about many things in her world. Trees were no longer vague green blobs: they now contained limbs from which clusters of individual leaves had sprung. A wall clock was no longer a blurred circle; she now saw hands and numbers on it. The full moon was not an indistinct glimmer but a clear shape like a silver coin.

Although Helen was amazed for a while as she readjusted her conception of the world, she did not resist the change. She took to her new learning willingly, for it cleared up a variety of situations that formerly had confused her and caused problems.

FAULTY DATA FROM FAULTY INFORMANTS

Much of what a child or youth learns about the world comes not from his own direct experience but from what he is told by others. If this information—passed to him from parents, from teachers, from peers, from books, from television—is innacurate and he believes it, he obviously will gain a faulty picture of life. The following case of a high-school sophomore illustrates the way a faulty informant affected one boy's life.

Darrell first brought himself to his English teacher's attention by a book report he wrote. In the novel that Darrell had read, there was a minor incident about a boy who ran away from home because of harsh treatment by his mother. The teacher was particularly curious about Darrell's report because he had ignored the main theme of the story and had dwelt at length on this brief passage, pointing out with considerable emotion that the character in the book would certainly deserve severe punishment for the sin of anger toward his parents. On a later occasion Darrell's report on another book again focused on a minor passage, this time one relating to the inner struggle of a youth who had experienced his first sexual feelings for a girl. In this case Darrell again said the boy was in danger because of his sinful thoughts. But Darrell also spent a paragraph building a defense for the boy who "could not always help what he thought."

One noon when the class was dismissed to go to lunch, Darrell remained in his seat with his head in his arms, quietly sobbing to himself. When the teacher asked what was wrong, Darrell was at first reluctant to talk, but then poured out his story. In gym class that morning he had been teased by his classmates when he had efused to hold any girl's hand in a square dance. The teacher asked why he felt this way about girls, and Darrell blurted forth a whole series of beliefs about what acts and thoughts are sinful and about how God punishes those who commit such acts.

Darrell, encouraged by the teacher's patience on this occasion, came several other times to talk through his worries. From these sessions the teacher was able to piece together the boy's pattern of beliefs which were causing him turmoil because they conflicted so with the ideas and behavior of many of his peers. As the teacher learned, Darrell's beliefs were mostly things told him by his mother.

The boy's home life had been somewhat unusual. His father had left home when Darrell was still an infant, so the boy had been raised entirely by his mother. She had provided an environment designed to encourage his artistic talents and protect him from "the wrong ideas." Darrell's spare time at home had always been taken up with drawing and painting, with practicing the piano and clarinet, with building airplane or automobile models, and with reading. Seldom had he played with other children except during recess at school and, when he was young, at Sunday school. Some of the beliefs which his mother had instilled in Darrell were:

Hate, violence, aggression, jealousy, fighting, conflict, and *dirty ideas* are all sinful. The "right kind of person" does not feel any of these, much less display them in his behavior. Life needs always to be calm and to be filled with moderation, love, and tolerance. A good child never feels anything but love and gratitude for others, especially for his mother who has sacrificed so much for him. Darrell's mother frequently pointed out that even though her husband had used her badly by abandoning her and her infant son, she forgave him and only felt a kindly tolerance for his weakness. In regard to relationships between the sexes, she emphasized that one should always avoid *dirty* thoughts. These were thoughts having to do with "feelings in our private parts and our minds" which were stimulated by such improper things as touching someone of the opposite sex, looking at photographs of scantily clad females, or listening to stories

about men and women "doing things." Since aggression an
violence of any kind should always be avoided—even thoughts c
violence—one should not engage in aggressive sports or look a
movies or read books containing fighting and conflict.

The English teacher felt that Darrell was suffering great guil
feelings because he had adopted the foregoing set of beliefs tha
conflicted with emotions of hate, sexual attraction, jealousy, ag
gression, and violence which naturally arise on certain occasion
for any normal person. In effect, Darrell's mother was serving a
a false prophet who was developing in the boy an unrealisti
superego. Darrell's map was built on false information.

OVERGENERALIZING FROM LIMITED EXPERIENCE

As noted earlier, a child may develop a view of life and a se
of adjustment techniques which are appropriate for one environ
ment but unsuitable for other environments. If the individua
fails to alter his perceptions to fit the new conditions, he find
himself maladjusted. This is the error of applying to all new situa
tions a generalization learned under one set of conditions. Th
mistake is that of not recognizing the ways in which the nev
situations differ from the old.

The case of Harlan illustrates this error of overgeneralizing
from limited experience. Harlan was a fifteen-year-old who hac
spent the past eleven years in a rather isolated area of the islanc
of Maui in the state of Hawaii. His father was manager of a
pineapple plantation. During these years Harlan had spent mos
of his time with his mother and two younger sisters, separatec
generally from the children of the other plantation employees
who were all of Oriental or Hawaiian ancestry. During most o
his school life, Harlan had not attended the local elementary
school but had been tutored by his mother, who had been a
teacher before her marriage.

On Maui, Harlan had grown up as a bookish boy with the
precise diction and advanced vocabulary his mother used and encouraged. He had become accustomed to ordering his sisters
around and correcting them when he thought they were in error.
Since there were two servants in his home, he had not learned to

make his own bed or clean his own room. In sum, he had learned to perceive himself as a privileged, well-read youth who knew more than other children and whose opinions were respected and encouraged by adults—with his mother and father serving as the principal models of adult behavior.

After Harlan finished the work of the eighth grade, he was sent to a boarding high school in Honolulu. In this new environment his adjustment troubles began. His customary perception of other people no longer fit. Reality had changed, but he kept trying to wrench the new reality to fit his familiar way of looking at life. His failure to accomplish this easily made him unhappy and confused. Too many things were different. The students were of various ethnic backgrounds, mostly of Japanese, Chinese, Korean, and Hawaiian stock. Although the children on the plantation had deferred to Harlan as the "white boss's son," these new schoolmates did not. Rather than respect his exalted speech habits, they laughed at him. Even worse, he was the least skilled of all the boys in physical activities. He had never played football, basketball, or baseball, so he was held in low esteem by his classmates who highly valued athletic prowess.

Although most of the teachers were Caucasians, they accorded him no special status. Instead, they criticized him for the negligent way he kept his room in the dormitory. His English teacher appeared to resent Harlan's habit of giving extended discourses in class about the authors and their works that were currently being studied.

In sum, Harlan had been well adjusted within his original environment, but when he moved to a new environment his original perceptions and adjustment techniques would no longer fulfill his needs.

AGE CHANGES IN EXPECTED BEHAVIOR

As a child grows up, society expects him continually to alter his behavior to suit his newest age level. In this case, the environment itself is ostensibly the same as always—the child lives in the same neighborhood with the same people around him—but the expectations of the people change. If a child does not realize this and accept it, he can find himself well adjusted by operating from one perception of reality, but later maladjusted without realizing why. The case of Brenda illustrates how this occurred in one girl's life.

At ages three and four Brenda was known as a "cute, curly-haired little thing" who constantly won the fond attention of her parents, grandparents, and their acquaintances. Since her retired grandfather lived next door, Brenda spent much of her time with him and with grandmother. One of Brenda's "cute" features was the normal baby-talk substitution of the *w* sound for the *l* and *r* (*little* became *wittow, run rabbit* became *wun wabbit*) and *f* for *th* (*thank you* became *fank oo*) or *d* for *th* (*there* became *dere*) and *th* for *s* (*seven* became *theven*). Her grandfather, for the amusement of guests, taught Brenda to recite alliterative verses ("Sister Suzy Sewing Shirts for Soldiers") and phrases ("Let's let the silly sailors stay"). Brenda had also won praise and laughter by making funny faces she had seen a television comic produce. She discovered that when her grandparents or parents became angry about something she had done, she could dissolve their anger into laughter by performing her funny-face act.

It was when Brenda was in first grade that her parents first became painfully aware that their daughter's baby talk and funny faces were no longer typical for her age. Adults who now saw her performance were more embarrassed than amused. When these behavior patterns persisted into second grade with little apparent change, Brenda's parents and grandparents became increasingly disturbed, particularly when they attended the PTA picnic and observed how much more mature the other children's speech was compared to Brenda's. Both the parents and grandparents now started a campaign to "make her grow up." They scolded and warned her to change her ways. This made her unhappy at home. At school some of the children mimicked her faces and speech, making her unhappy there also. In brief, she was a victim of the fact that adjustment techniques considered appropriate for one age level may be considered unsuitable at another.

In conclusion, we note again that a person may find himself maladjusted either because he originally developed a faulty view of the world or because the perceptions he developed to suit one environment are no longer appropriate when he moves into another or when he moves to a new age level. To solve this problem of an inappropriate life-view he needs to develop a truer perception of current conditions and more suitable adjustment techniques.

HELPING PUPILS REVISE THEIR LEARNING

Although psychologists for many years have investigated the questions "What is learning?" and "How do people learn?" they have not yet arrived at very complete answers. Even so, laboratory research and the experience of educators and clinicians have furnished some useful guidelines for assisting the maladjusted student in learning more adequate views of life and more suitable ways of behaving. In the remainder of this chapter we shall discuss a series of generalizations which may serve as such guidelines. The generalizations are presented under three headings, each of which describes a basic step in the process of revising past learnings: (1) motivation to change, (2) perception of alternative behaviors, and (3) trial and effect.

MOTIVATION TO CHANGE

A person is willing to change his present perceptions of life or his present adjustment techniques only if he is sufficiently dissatisfied with the way his needs are fulfilled. Though this is a rather obvious fact, it is sometimes overlooked by school personnel. The teacher may well be ignoring it when he remarks with dismay: "Why doesn't that boy study more?" or "Why does she continue to run around with that gang?" or "I told him what the consequences would be, and still he keeps acting up." What the teacher fails to recognize is that in many cases these students are simply not sufficiently dissatisfied with their lot to alter their way of life. If the teacher could see life from their perspective, he would understand.

This fuel for accomplishing personality changes which we have termed *dissatisfaction* is known by a variety of other names as well: motivation, unhappiness, anxiety, desire, ambition, misery, aspiration, hope, yearning, wishing, wanting. All of them have one factor in common: a discrepancy between (1) the individual's needs and (2) the degree to which the needs are being met.

Like most things, dissatisfaction or motivation comes in different amounts. Before a person is willing to change his ways of handling his life, his feeling of dissatisfaction must have reached a high enough level to warrant the trouble it will take for him to accomplish the change. If the required change is minor, a little dissatisfaction may suffice to stimulate it. But if the change involves much trouble or discomfort or psychological risk, a large measure of unhappiness, ambition, anxiety, or desire will be required to bring it about.

This relationship between the amount of change needed and the amount of dissatisfaction required to accomplish it is of considerable importance to the teacher, since he himself sometimes must serve as an agent that motivates—a fomenter of dissatisfaction—before the student will attempt to change. Some pupils come to the teacher or counselor with sufficient drive or desire or ambition or misery to activate the change. Their problem is that they do not know the method for accomplishing it. The teacher's or counselor's task in these cases is only to demonstrate suitable methods to make the alteration. But other pupils who are maladjusted do not yet have sufficient motivation to accomplish the improvement in their condition, so they need both: motivation and guidance to find new methods that will better satisfy their needs.

Two practical questions now arise for the teacher: (1) Under what circumstances should a teacher or counselor consciously try to increase a pupil's dissatisfaction with himself? (2) What techniques will best foment a constructive discontent in the pupil?

To answer the first of these questions, a teacher may be guided by two principal criteria or generalizations:

1. *A teacher should not try to make a student dissatisfied with himself unless the student has a reasonable chance of accomplishing the necessary change.* To whet the student's appetite for pleasures he can never obtain simply increases his maladjustment. To shame him for shortcomings which he can never correct only makes him more distraught. Even though this criterion seems self-evident, we mention it here because teachers and parents

often ignore it in their treatment of children and youth. They harangue the mentally slow child to do better academically, despite the fact that he lacks the capacity to do their bidding. They may confront the emotionally distraught youth with his personality shortcomings at a time when his inner turmoil prevents him from making a reasonable attempt to correct them. Thus, if the teacher estimates that the pupil's present condition renders him unable to solve his problem no matter how strongly he might be motivated by dissatisfaction, the teacher would do well not to make the pupil more anxious than he is. Rather, the pupil may need to learn to accept the inevitable; so, in handling him, the teacher may wish to show she accepts him as he is and is not trying to change him.

However, if the counselor or teacher believes that greater effort on the student's part would enable the student to achieve a better solution to his problems than he is currently achieving, the teacher is warranted in stimulating the student to greater dissatisfaction with himself.

2. *The goal toward which the teacher motivates the student should promise satisfaction for the student from his own viewpoint, not just from the teacher's perception of life.* That is, the teacher should not impose his own goals or standards on the student when the student's ambitions, though different, might be as acceptable to society and more suitable to his style of life and values than are the teacher's. This matter of the suitability of goals is treated later in some detail, so we only mention it here as an issue to keep in mind when deciding whether to try making a pupil discontented with his current condition. (See Chapter 7: Individuality Versus Maladjustment.)

Now to the second question posed above: What techniques will best foment a constructive discontent in the pupil?

The technique that will be most appropriate for a particular student depends upon a variety of factors in his life: his perception of himself and of the teacher, his intellectual abilities, the frustrations he currently faces in life, his past experiences with parents and teachers, and the like. Thus, we cannot validly suggest techniques that will suit all pupils. Instead, we can review some of the popular approaches in order to illustrate the variety of techniques from which a teacher may draw. Then we will suggest criteria that may aid a teacher in determining whether the discontent created by these devices is "constructive."

School marks are probably the most common tools teachers use for causing student dissatisfaction. Test grades, marks on compositions and work products, and grades on report cards will serve to alert pupils to their shortcomings. Teachers not only use current grades as stimulators of discontent, but they frequently use the threat—direct or implied—of low marks in the future to motivate changed behavior. Other threatened punishments include additional homework, staying after school, writing the same sentence several hundred times, sitting in the principal's office, losing recreational and athletic privileges, being dismissed from school, and the like.

Another way to prompt self-dissatisfaction in students is to furnish them a reflection of the way their shortcomings appear to others. The student who is unaware that his voice is strident or his enunciation is unclear can become more aware of these characteristics if he hears a tape recording of his speech. A photograph helps him see his posture as others do. Video tapes, which some schools experiment with today, furnish the pupil with a television version of his speech and actions.

A student may become more aware of his shortcomings if classmates are asked to furnish an appraisal of his oral report or of his performance on a debate team. In a physical-education class pupils may rate each other on a good-sportsmanship scale and thus alert each other to personality characteristics as viewed by teammates.

In addition to fostering dissatisfaction by focusing on student shortcomings in the foregoing ways, teachers may also adopt the more positive tacks of opening new vistas and of stressing elements of strength in the pupil's behavior. For example, during a study of vocations, the teacher may illustrate a series of occupational opportunities which students had never realized would be open to them. As a result, the students become dissatisfied with their present goals and adopt more ambitious ones. This same positive type of dissatisfaction can be produced by a teacher's making the student aware that the student has an aptitude which, if further developed, would be highly valued by the world—a talent for athletics, for science, for art, for writing, for debating, for mechanics, and so on.

Sometimes the most important factor in stimulating a student is a teacher's sincere, personal interest in the student's welfare. After the teacher has demonstrated his friendly concern, the student often tries to alter his present style of life to become more the kind of person he believes the teacher would respect.

Now that we have identified the foregoing variety of ways to foment dissatisfaction, we turn to the next question: Which of these techniques are the most constructive and effective?

We cannot suggest a universally correct answer, for the complex of factors playing upon a student is different in one case than it is in another. We can, however, suggest one rather apparent criterion that should be kept in mind when a method of motivating the pupil is being selected. The criterion is this: *the technique should stimulate the pupil to work toward the desired goal, but it should not at the same time produce side effects that are more disturbing than the pupil's original condition.* In other words, the cure should not be worse than the original malady. For example, some pupils who receive low marks on tests or report cards rise to the challenge and by working hard bring up the marks so their adjustment is enhanced. But some other kinds of pupils become so discouraged by low grades that they end up rejecting all schooling. Thus their ultimate adjustment is worse than ever. Furthermore, teachers or parents sometimes shame a child into working harder in school by comparing him unfavorably with his classmates, but this improvement in schoolwork is accompanied by such unwelcome behavioral changes as chronic cheating or lying, bitterness toward adults, or feelings of great shame and depression. Hence, when a teacher stimulates dissatisfaction in the student, the teacher should be alert to the side effects which his methods may have generated and should be ready to adopt a different tack if the side effects are producing further maladjustment for the student.

PERCEPTION OF ALTERNATIVE BEHAVIORS

It seems almost self-evident that a person who is displeased with his present condition would much prefer to have the world change to suit him rather than to have to change himself to fit the world. In short, personality change requires energy, trouble, and risk of failure. So, one's first reaction to maladjustment is to blame the environment and expect it to change. But when the environment will not do so, one must face the reality that his happiness will result only if he alters his own approach to life. At this point of accepting the necessity of change, the student needs to see what alternative behaviors are possible.

In the classroom there are many opportunities for demonstrating alternative behaviors. One way is for the teacher to use examples from incidents around the school, from literary selections, and from newspapers as foci of discussions. For example, teachers may initiate the consideration of alternative behaviors in different situations by asking such questions as the following:

> How is this incident in the lunchroom like the story we read the other day about *The Boy Who Cried "Wolf"*?
>
> What might Hamlet have done instead of trying to avenge his father's death? And if he had taken this alternative course, how might the results have been different?
>
> Ralph, you said that in the story we just read, Comstock was meddlesome. You said he shouldn't have interfered with other peoples' business. Yet the other day we discussed an incident in the newspaper telling of a woman being beaten in a parking lot, and none of the neighbors or passersby came to aid her. How would you suggest we decide when to meddle and when not to?

In addition to the foregoing type of general consideration of alternative acts, there are also opportunities for the teacher to guide a particular student into adopting more satisfactory adjustment techniques. There are various ways to approach this task. Perhaps the most common is for the teacher to list alternatives for the student:

> Diane, instead of punching her, next time you could let the umpire handle the problem, or you could just turn your back and walk away—leaving her standing there looking silly.
>
> Carl, why not do the Spanish homework right after you get

home, and then play for a while? After supper you could do the arithmetic and spelling assignments. That way you could get the work done and still be in bed on time.

However, some teachers and counselors are not enthusiastic about giving direct advice. They feel that such suggestions too often are forgotten by the emotionally distraught student or are ignored by the one who resists adult efforts to influence him. These educators, therefore, prefer to lead the student himself to describe new possibilities for action. Thus their discussions may contain questions like:

What do you think you might do next time so that you can give the book report without becoming so frightened that you forget what you were going to say?

What other ways might you be able to get money for the bike?

TRIAL AND EFFECT

The next two steps in the revision of past, inadequate learnings consist of (1) having the pupil try a new behavior so that (2) he can experience its successful effects. The interrelationship between these two steps has often been demonstrated in learning experiments. The learning process can be described briefly in these terms: First, the individual is motivated to action by unfulfilled needs. Second, he has in mind a repertoire of alternative behaviors by which he might try to fulfill the needs. From these alternatives he selects the top priority—the act he believes will best accomplish the job—and he tries this out. If this approximation or trial succeeds, its position on the priority list is raised or strengthened. In a similar situation in the future when the needs arise, it is now even more likely that the individual will turn again to this behavior rather than one of the other possibilities. But if the trial has failed, or has brought less success than he had hoped, the chances that he will use that behavior again in similar circumstances are reduced. Failure causes an alternative behavior to drop to a lower position on the priority list.

Therefore, after a teacher ensures that the student is motivated and that he is aware of alternative behaviors, it is the teacher's next problem to ensure that the pupil actually attempts the most desirable of the new behaviors so that he can experience success. Again, it is the experience of success—the positive effect—that securely builds the new behavior or adjustment technique into the pupil's style of life.

This next step—ensuring that the student tries the new behavior—is often difficult to accomplish, for the student breaks away from his old habit patterns only at the risk of failing with the new attempt. It is particularly difficult for the teacher to encourage the insecure, fearful child to attempt something new. This is because the child usually has experienced a long series of failures when he has tried the unfamiliar. He has learned that it is better to stick with his present, though somewhat unsatisfactory, way of doing things than it is to court even greater disaster by striking out in untested directions.

Not only does the teacher face the problem of convincing the child to take the chance of attempting the new, but he faces the further problems that may occur if the child's first attempt is clumsy and yields a less-than-satisfactory result. When a pupil's first trials are unrewarding, he becomes even less enthusiastic about risking another similar attempt. To obviate this problem of sponsoring unsuccessful first trials, the teacher tries to arrange the learning situation so the pupil's initial approximation will yield a positive result, at least to some degree. A pupil who is thus rewarded by success is willing to risk another and perhaps better approximation in the future. When a complex form of behavior is involved, this cycle (approximating the new behavior, experiencing some success, correcting the shortcomings, then trying a new version of the behavior, experiencing more success, etc.) is repeated over and over as the individual develops refined, sophisticated patterns of action.

What, then, are some of the ways that teachers can encourage pupils to attempt new adjustment techniques and thus experience the success that will bring these new techniques more securely into the pupils' habit patterns?

To answer this, we shall describe briefly some of the methods teachers have found useful. In the final four chapters of the book these methods are illustrated by means of case studies.

Perhaps the most common method teachers use is verbal encouragement or challenge. They may say to the student, "I'm sure you could do it" or "Just give it one try" or "I have a lot of faith in your ability." This appeal is usually most successful when the student admires the teacher and is thus willing to risk trying the new act in order to earn the teacher's approval. A high-school student, speaking of his English teacher who used this approach, said, "She treats us as if we had all kinds of ability. So in order not to disappoint her, we work as hard as we can and end up accomplishing more than we even thought we could." Though this technique is often effective, it is inappropriate if the change the pupil is to make is too complex for him to manage or if his fears of attempting the change are too great.

When the new behavior the student is to adopt is too complex for his abilities, the teacher can sometimes aid by dismantling the behavior patterns into constituent subacts. The student may be willing to take the smaller risk of trying one or two subacts, though he would have been overwhelmed if confronted by the entire complex. For instance, the speech correctionist can often analyze a child's faulty speech pattern into subtasks and successfully encourage the child to improve one of these before even drawing the pupil's attention to the fact that other aspects of his speech are also unsatisfactory.

In many cases the student is aided in attempting a new behavior by being provided safe practice conditions before he must try the behavior under real-life conditions. For example, the teacher may want the student to learn more appropriate ways to respond to criticism in various life situations. The teacher and student might begin working on the problem by discussing how one might react to criticism and what the consequences of such reactions might be. To move closer to the actual lifelike conditions, the teacher might then propose a simulated situation in which the teacher and student assume the roles of antagonists in criticism. "Imagine I'm your math teacher. I've accused you of copying homework from another classmate, and I have evidence to support my accusation. What would you do or say if I told you, 'I'm not counting this homework assignment, because it's clear that you didn't do your own work'?" Thus the teacher has moved from the unemotionalized discussion stage to the more lifelike acting-out stage which requires the student to react spontaneously to another individual's behavior and, as a consequence, to experience some of the emotional components of real-life conditions. The sociodrama permits the student to make errors without having to suffer the true-life consequences of his mistakes. Thus, he is better prepared to face similar situations when they arise in his life, and he is familiar enough with adequate response patterns to use them in place of his old inadequate ones.

Sometimes students become willing to adopt new behaviors when they have seen someone else, in conditions similar to their own, succeed with these behaviors. There are numerous sources of models for such action. Books, motion pictures, television dramas, and plays all furnish possibilities for the youth. For example, a physically handicapped girl may read the biography of an individual who suffered a disability similar to her own, and she may thus be stimulated to attempt some of the adjustment techniques which the character in the book found profitable.

Schoolmates sometimes stimulate a hesitant pupil to adopt a new pattern of action. If the pupil does not automatically recognize that he might model his own behavior after that of a suitable age-mate, the teacher may help him recognize this by saying something like "Jim is no larger or stronger than you, and he's out there in the game. If he can do it, you can." Classmates can effectively support the overly cautious child in his first attempts by saying, "Come on, Dana, you can do it. We'll be with you if you need help."

The foregoing approaches, then, may encourage the pupil to attempt a new view of life or a new method of adjustment. But once he makes the attempt, the teacher should help ensure that he is suitably rewarded for his effort. In many instances the reward is quite evident to the student, so the teacher need not meddle. That is, the goal the pupil sought has been reached—he has passed the history test, he has successfully completed the public address that he had feared, or he has courageously asked the girl to dance. But in many other instances the results are indeterminate or mixed (partially successful, partially unsuccessful) or are interpreted by the student as failure because he had expected to achieve much more. In other words, the student is often an inadequate or unsure judge of his own performance, so he must depend on outside evaluators to appraise his work. In such cases it is proper for the teacher to point out to the student the positive results of his trial effort so the student will be encouraged toward making similar efforts in the future. Sometimes the teacher can accomplish this by giving a general expression of approval like "Good job" or "You're coming along fine" or "You can be proud of yourself." But the teacher's reaction serves as a more useful guide to future behavior if the strong aspects of the performance are specified and are shown in proper relation to the aspects that still warrant improvement.

Betty, I don't know if you realize how much better you were this time in presenting your oral report. You had your ideas well organized, and you spoke out clearly. We had no trouble hearing you in any part of the room. I could see you were disappointed in not being able to answer all the questions the class asked. But don't worry about that. You did a good job. And for the next report I'll work with you ahead of time to outline the questions they probably will ask, and you'll be all set for them.

In sum, the teacher uses whatever methods he can find for stimulating the maladjusted student to try new, more adequate types of behavior. Once the new, more suitable behavior has been tried, the teacher attempts to ensure that the student is rewarded for his efforts so that he will adopt an appropriate variety of the new behavior in the future when faced with similar situations. In other words, *the feeling of reward has the effect of raising a new perception or new adjustment technique to a higher availability level in the student's repertoire of acts.*

Summary
A student may find himself maladjusted either because he originally developed a faulty view of the world or because the perceptions he developed to suit one environment are no longer

appropriate when he moves into another or when he moves to a new age level. To solve this problem, he needs to develop a truer perception of current conditions and more suitable adjustment techniques.

Before he will change his perceptions or adjustment techniques, he must be sufficiently dissatisfied with the way his needs are currently fulfilled and must perceive other, more appropriate alternative ways of acting. Then he must try one or more of these alternatives. If he feels his first trial has brought him somewhat closer to his goal than his old behavior patterns had, he will tend to supplant the old with the new. If his first trial is insufficiently rewarding, he will abandon this new form of action and revert to his old habits or else try some other new alternative.

CHAPTER 4

IMPROVING THE ENVIRONMENT

To orient ourselves once again to the introductory remarks from Chapter 3, we note that a maladjusted person becomes better adjusted if:

1. He learns new ways to perceive life and new techniques for handling life's problems, or

2. His environment changes so it better fits the adjustment techniques he is accustomed to using, or

3. Both 1 and 2.

Chapter 4 offers a brief overview of what the school can do to change a student's environment in order to improve his adjustment. The discussion treats changes that may be made through administrative measures, classroom teaching methods, influencing parents, and appealing to extramural agencies.

ADMINISTRATIVE MEASURES

The school has a variety of ways of altering the student's academic environment. One of the most familiar is to retain (flunk or fail) him in the same grade another year in hopes that he will make a better adjustment if he covers the same material a second time. Although some pupils do profit from retention at the same grade level, studies of this problem have shown that most students who have been retained would have been better off if they had moved ahead with their age-mates.[1] Of course, in many cases in which a student is held back because he has done poorly, the school officials are focusing more on maintaining the school's scholastic standards than they are on providing the most compatible environment for the learner.

One method of altering the very apt student's environment is to accelerate him beyond his age-mates. Acceleration—sometimes called skipping—usually means pushing him a half grade or whole

[1] R. Murray Thomas and Shirley M. Thomas. *Individual Differences in the Classroom.* New York: David McKay Co., 1965, p. 123.

45

grade ahead. This method works well if the student is not only academically able but is also advanced physically and socially so that he is a well-rounded, mature match for the students in his new class. Acceleration also succeeds best if the pupil has been aided in catching up with the essential materials which his new classmates studied prior to his promotion into their class.

Another approach to fitting the academic environment to pupils' varied talents is ability grouping, sometimes called homogeneous or cluster grouping. This consists of placing children of similar academic potential in the same class. For instance, if a ninth grade is composed of six sections of students, those with the best past performance in mathematics will be assigned together in one classroom, those with the next-best record to another, and so on until the least successful pupils are placed in the sixth section. Likewise, in physical-education classes pupils are homogeneously grouped according to athletic ability or such physical criteria as height and weight. To care for academically gifted students, some schools either provide special advanced classes or permit the best students in the highest classes of the high school to attend one or two classes at a nearby college.

The school may also offer special classes for pupils suffering handicaps like mental retardation, blindness, speech and hearing disabilities, and such educational difficulties as retardation in reading, arithmetic, and writing.

In recent years the nongraded school has become a popular administrative mechanism for adapting the environment to learners' needs. A nongraded school (sometimes referred to as *ungraded* or *continuous-promotion* school) does not identify classes by specific grade-level designations. Instead, a more general term, like *primary block* or *intermediate unit,* is applied to a class. Within a primary block one seven-year-old may be working on prereading tasks typical of the work faced by advanced kindergarten children in traditional schools whereas another more apt seven-year-old may be reading typical third-grade books. In brief, the nongraded classroom provides opportunities for pupils to work at a level of difficulty suited to their individual talents, yet the pupil's work need not be identified publicly by a grade designation.

Parallel-track plans are common in high schools. With these, a student is enrolled in a particular track or stream that represents a series of courses composing a curriculum. One track may be labeled *college preparatory*, another *vocational*, a third *business*, a fourth *general*, and a fifth *home economics*. The purpose of the tracks is to offer curricula appropriate to different students' abilities and vocational goals.

CLASSROOM TEACHING METHODS

The obvious, though oft ignored, principle governing the adaptation of classroom methods to individual pupils' needs is: Do not insist that everyone do the identical task at the same time, but adjust tasks and classroom groupings as much as possible to individuals' abilities and stages of learning.

At this point we shall only suggest in a general way the variety of possibilities for adapting classroom procedures to help pupils achieve better adjustment. We shall postpone until the final four chapters a description of specific adaptations to fit the needs of particular pupils.

Within the classroom the students can be regrouped so that all are not studying the same thing in the same way at the same time. Instead, learning tasks are adapted to student differences in skill, interest, and need.

Sometimes these groupings are formal and permanent. In many elementary-school classrooms teachers place pupils in three or four reading groups, each group suited to the reading maturity of the pupils in it. Throughout the year a child usually stays in the same group for his daily reading activities. Likewise, in high-school physical-education classes students are frequently divided into teams on the basis of skill, size, and strength.

In other cases, however, groups are formed only on a temporary basis to fulfill an immediate need. In a high-school English class the pupils who showed that they still did not understand how to outline a composition properly may be drawn together for two class periods to review outlining procedures and receive intensive practice. In this same class the most apt students who have finished their outlining assignments early may form a group that writes radio scripts portraying incidents in the lives of authors they have been studying. On another occasion the students who continue to confuse the nominative and objective cases in the use of *who* and *whom* may be drawn together for a portion of a class period to review this topic.

Many schools provide opportunities for two or three pupils to be withdrawn from a class for a segment of time to meet in another room with a teacher who will provide special help, such as in remedial reading or in remedial speech.

Teachers may often accomplish the purpose of subgrouping— adjusting to individual students' needs—without dividing the class in a physical sense. Rather than cluster different groups of pupils in different sections of the room, the teacher creates the divisions in his own mind. Only close observation of his treatment of individuals will reveal that he has made distinctions among class members. A history teacher may assign an academically apt student an advanced book on the Civil War and assign a less able scholar a simpler book on the same topic. A science teacher, when conducting an oral-question session with the class, may aim the more difficult questions at the most gifted pupils and the easier questions at slower learners. An English instructor may apply more sophisticated standards when commenting on a very able student's composition than he does when marking the less able student's work.

New teaching materials developed in recent years provide a way to suit learning tasks to individual pupils, yet permit all members of the class to pursue the same activity at the same time. Most of these materials are of the programed-learning variety. In most cases a special form of a book or a teaching machine presents each student a graduated series of small learning segments. The student reads the first segment, answers a question about it, and is immediately informed—by the next page in the book or the next frame shown on the machine—how accurate his answer has been. The student then reads the next segment, answers a question, and learns of the accuracy of his answer. This process continues through the course of learning so that each student is studying the same topics as his classmates, but he is doing so at his own speed. The development of such individualized materials is significantly expanding the classroom teacher's repertoire of ways to alter the learning environment to suit individual learners.

Variations of the foregoing techniques for adapting classroom teaching to pupils' adjustment needs are illustrated in the twenty-one case studies that compose Part Three.

INFLUENCING PARENTS

In a great number of cases of child maladjustment, the main trouble lies in the home. If some alterations could be made in the family environment, the child could live a much more satisfactory life. Some parents are too strict; others are too lax. Some over-protect the child; others neglect him. One parent may treat the child coldly and the other smother him with affection. They may hold him to standards of achievement which he can never reach, or they may fail to teach him any sense of responsibility. One child may be confused and ashamed because his parents are divorced. Another may feel unwanted because his parents so obviously prefer a sibling to him. Some homes fail their children by not furnishing a nutritious diet or proper medical and dental care. These and scores of other domestic inadequacies may be primary causes of a child's or youth's psychological disturbance.

Whether a teacher or counselor can ameliorate such unsatisfactory home circumstances usually depends upon his ability to influence the pupil's parents. Some parents are readily influenced. They are eager to improve their child-raising practices. They will go to great effort and expense to carry out the teacher's recommendations. Many other adults, however, reject any implication that they are less than adequate parents. They resent school personnel who try to alter their ways of raising their children. Still other mothers and fathers are eager to improve the child's home conditions, but because of their own financial, marital, or psychological limitations, they cannot.

Often a teacher may conclude that certain pupils would be much better off if placed in a different home, but such placement is rarely possible. Only under extreme circumstances will the courts authorize the removal of a child from his own family. And even if he is removed, there is no guarantee that a suitable home can be provided for him. The fact is that many children must continue living in family circumstances that are contrary to their welfare.

Though the teacher may be able to do nothing to alter unsatisfactory home conditions, he sometimes can supply some of the elements missing in the student's life. To some degree, teachers may play the roles of friendly counselor, affectionate friend, unshockable listener to the youth's emotional troubles, and the like.

APPEALING TO EXTRAMURAL AGENCIES

A final way the school may affect the child's environment is by soliciting the help of outside agencies. The aid of the Big Brother organization can be sought to provide occasional adult male companionship for the boy who has no father. A child guidance clinic may agree to work with the pupil and his parents over an extended period of time to effect a better relationship among them. The county welfare and medical organizations can furnish financial and medical assistance to impoverished families. Children who might profit from club and recreation programs can be enrolled in the Boy or Girl Scouts, the Campfire Girls, the YMCA or YWCA, and Catholic and Jewish youth organizations. Students from a local college can be asked to tutor culturally deprived elementary and high-school pupils. Local employment agencies and men's service organizations like the Kiwanis and Lions clubs can assist in finding jobs for high-school youth.

In sum, most communities contain a broad spectrum of agencies whose aid the school can enlist for changing the environments in which maladjusted pupils exist.

Summary

Oftentimes a child or youth can achieve better personal-social adjustment if changes are made in his environment. To some extent the school can adapt the environment to the student through administrative measures like homogeneous grouping or different curriculum tracks, through individualizing classroom teaching methods, through suggestions to parents for changes at home, and through securing the help of other agencies in the community.

Part Two

THE TEACHER'S ROLE

If a teacher is to aid disturbed individuals and at the same time help a roomful of other students acquire academic skills, he needs to recognize: (1) the limitations which he should place on the results he expects because of the nature of his training and his teaching responsibilities, (2) feasible methods of identifying maladjusted students, and (3) a process which he may adopt to aid maladjusted students within the school setting. Part Two treats these three facets of the teacher's role as a counselor.

CHAPTER 5

TEACHER VERSUS CLINICIAN

Today's teachers are better equipped to recognize the reasons for personality problems than were teachers several decades ago. It is the psychologist who deserves much of the credit for sensitizing teachers to the social-psychological disturbances that pupils suffer. But the psychologist also deserves the blame for causing teachers unreasonable guilt feelings. As he has sensitized educators to the factors that affect the child's personality development, he frequently has neglected to make clear the difference between the role of the teacher and that of the clinician. Consequently many teachers have adopted for themselves unreasonable expectations about what they should be accomplishing with disturbed children.

Perhaps the distinctions between the clinician's and teacher's roles can be indicated most succinctly by the following chart.

THE TYPICAL CLINICIAN	THE TYPICAL TEACHER
His Primary Responsibility	
To discover the underlying causes for an individual's personal-social difficulties, then to guide him toward rebuilding his personality and/or toward developing a new relationship between himself and his environment.	To teach a group of youths (who have varied abilities and personality characteristics) a series of specified skills and information deemed appropriate for their age level. The teaching is intended to form the students into intelligent citizens who will function skillfully and diligently in vocations and in family life.
His Work Load	
Five or six children a day. He sees each child or youth individually for about an hour.	At the elementary-school level, 30 to 35 children a day, five or six hours a day for an

53

His Work Load—Cont'd

Each may come once a week or more, usually over a period of several months or a year or more.

eight- or nine-month school year. At the secondary-school level, 120 to 180 youths a day in groups of about 30, for 40 minutes a day for one or two semesters.

His Psychological Training

Between 15 and 25 college courses in psychology and allied subjects (sociology, juvenile delinquency, brain physiology, etc.), including guided practice in psychological testing, interviewing, and psychotherapy.

Between one and three courses in psychology, usually of a survey nature rather than courses stressing analysis of individuals' personality problems.

The foregoing comparison suggests that the typical teacher has the training and time to offer only a modicum of aid toward the solution of disturbed students' problems. Therapy for deep-seated difficulties is the responsibility of the psychiatrist or clinical psychologist. Aid with less serious problems is the task of the school's counseling staff. Help with improving the pupil's home environment is the job of the social worker. The classroom teacher, as he guides pupils toward skills and subject-matter goals, can be expected to offer minor aid toward improving pupils' personal-social adjustment, but he should not feel guilty because he is unable to rebuild disturbed students' personalities or to readjust their family relationships.

As noted above, certain psychologists have caused teachers to assume too much responsibility for students' personality problems and home environment. Other clinicians, however, have recommended quite the opposite. They have told educators to limit themselves to teaching skills and subject matter and to avoid completely students' personal-social problems. They have warned that teachers with little or no training as therapists may do more harm than good in attempting to treat students' psychological difficulties—difficulties which are often quite complex. This warning is appropriate if it means that teachers should refrain from attempting depth analysis and complex therapy with markedly disturbed pupils. But it is foolish if it means that teachers should do nothing which may affect pupils' personal-social adjustment, since such a warning simply cannot be heeded. Because the disturbed pupil is in the classroom each day, the instructor is forced to interact with him. The child inevitably is affected if the instructor ignores him rather than calls upon him to recite or if the instructor sympathizes with him rather than criticizing his acts, is sarcastic rather than friendly, expects him to fulfill assignments rather than excusing him from work, and so on. Thus, since the teacher cannot avoid influencing children's personality development, it is important that he gain as much psychological understanding as possible so that his influence will be on the side of wisdom.

Summary

The classroom instructor is not responsible for solving serious personality problems and the family difficulties of disturbed pupils. He is, however, responsible for cooperating with the in-school aspects of a program of treatment set up for markedly disturbed pupils who are undergoing therapy in a clinic. Furthermore, in his daily work the teacher is responsible for making estimates of the needs of his pupils so that he may treat them in ways that will promote their personal-social adjustment.

CHAPTER 6

IDENTIFYING DISTURBED STUDENTS

When a clinical psychologist or psychiatrist assesses personal-social adjustment, he typically utilizes four sources of information: (1) direct observation of the patient's behavior, (2) extensive interviews with the patient, (3) reports of other people's observations of the patient, and (4) psychological test results. The teacher, on the other hand, usually confines himself to observations of the student and to conversations with him. A typical teacher has neither the time nor training to use such specialized appraisal devices as the Rorschach Test, dream analysis, word association tests, and the like. And even the observations and interviews which he is prepared to make must often be cursory. Particularly at the secondary-school level, where an instructor faces as many as 120 to 180 pupils a day, the teacher's routine instructional duties are so demanding that he has little time for more than a superficial impression of most students' adjustment. Usually it is feasible for him to study carefully only those few students who bring themselves to his attention because they seem to need special aid. At the elementary-school level, a more manageable 30 to 35 pupils a day enable the teacher to develop a deeper understanding of each child.

The following discussion of appraisal techniques is made with these realities of the typical classroom and the typical teacher in mind. The teacher is not a therapist responsible for only a few patients. As noted in Chapter 5, his main assignment is to guide a large group toward school goals—goals which are usually more academic than personal-social. As much as possible the instructor's judgments about personality adjustment must be made by means of techniques that can be a part of his teaching routine. His judgments are based primarily on his own observations of a pupil's behavior in the classroom, secondarily on the observations of others who know the pupil, and very slightly on the results of formal personality tests. We shall inspect each of these techniques in some detail.

OBSERVATIONS

The two aspects of observing that are of most importance to teachers are: (1) the kinds of behavior worth observing and (2) the most feasible ways of collecting observations.

WHAT IS WORTH OBSERVING?

Our earlier inspection of a personality theory serves as our guide to answering the question: What is worth observing? By watching the student we try to estimate: (1) how well he fulfills his responsibilities to society and how well he lives according to the rules, (2) how well he satisfies his needs, (3) the form of his superego and how well he meets its demands, and (4) the structure of his ego, that is, the accuracy of the mental map that he has constructed to represent reality. As we discuss each of these we shall pose some of the questions teachers can keep in mind to guide their observations of pupils.

Adjustment to Society

Of the four aspects, this is the easiest to assess. The citizenship or deportment sections of report cards contain some of the questions about this facet which schools usually consider important: Does he follow school rules? Does he hand in assignments on time? Does he complete his fair share of the work on group projects? Does he respect other people's property and their right to make their own decisions? Does he voluntarily give aid to those who need it?

In addition to these formally stated expectations of society, there are a host of informal ones which have become part of the culture. One problem that occurs with these unstated expectations is that they are not accepted equally by all segments of society. One expectation may be embraced by one subgroup of society (such as the upper-middle class of American society or the members of the Catholic church) but rejected by another. This leaves the school's personnel in the position of deciding which of the conflicting social values to support. The teacher usually ends up supporting those values which he himself holds. For example, as a member of the middle class, the teacher may approve of pupils who conform to, and may disapprove of those who violate, the following kinds of unstated standards:

When boys fight, they do not hit below the belt, do not bite or scratch, and do not hit the opponent once he is down.

When a rule or custom is violated and the teacher asks who did it, the pupil who violated the rule should admit it and not try to cast blame on others.

Students should neither display nor manipulate their genitals nor, in the case of older girls, their breasts.

When a pupil makes a request or receives a favor or disturbs someone, he should show his respect for others by using such terms as *please, thank you, I appreciate it very much,* and *I beg your pardon.*

Psychologists and social workers have sometimes observed that teachers would be of greater service to the pupils from the lower socioeconomic strata by understanding these children's home backgrounds and parental expectations and by not insisting such pupils adhere to middle-class standards in so many respects.

In sum, a student's adjustment to society is estimated through observations of how closely he hews to both the formal and informal expectations of his school society.

Satisfaction of Personal Needs

This facet of adjustment is much more difficult to appraise than the foregoing one, because a person may hide from the world his unfulfilled inner drives or yearnings. Even so, an alert teacher can often make astute guesses about inner needs from observations of pupil behavior. This is usually easier to do in the primary grades than in the high school, because the younger the child, the less adept he tends to be at masking feelings and the less aware he is that society disapproves of so many of his desires. Two types of behavior that may reveal unsatisfied needs are direct statements and persistent extraordinary behavior.

Direct statements of needs: Some children do not hide their yearnings but voice them to the teacher or to classmates. In some instances they express their opinions frankly during regular class sessions, such as, "I would like to do important things in school, like lead the singing or be an office messenger, but you never choose me." In other instances they maintain their silence in class but during individual conversations with the teacher they lower their protective facade to say, "I never seem to be good at anything, and I feel terrible about it." Or "I want awfully much to have boyfriends like the other girls, but the right kinds of boys don't seem to like me."

Persistent extraordinary behavior: Some pupils are very shy. They avoid making overtures to others, and they hesitate to attempt new activities. Some show inordinate fears: they are afraid of physical activities, of saying the wrong thing in class, of meeting strangers, and the like. Others always try to draw attention to themselves by acting up or by talking loudly or by misbehaving. Some always welcome a dare to risk their life or reputation. Some are constantly sensitive to any remark which might be considered a criticism, and they hasten to attack the one who criticizes them. Each of these extremes of behavior *may* be a symptom of ineffective need satisfaction. The overly shy person's retiring behavior may be preventing him from fulfilling needs for affection and companionship. The overly aggressive one may desire self-respect and status in others' eyes. The pupil who is compulsive about being neat and clean may need parental affection which he lacks but which he believes can be won only by his being inordinately "good and clean."

Therefore, by observing what pupils say directly about their needs and noting how they act in class and on the play field, the teacher is able to improve his estimate of how well their inner needs are being met.

Nature of the Superego

Although some philosophers and religious leaders have believed that humans are born knowing right from wrong, this belief is not widely held today by social scientists. They believe instead that the ideals, moral values, and rules which guide a person's life are learned from his environment, from incorporating the values of his family and community into his personality. In some cases the values he adopts are not well suited either (1) to the society in which he must live or in which he aspires to live or (2) to the needs that arise within him.

Superego and society: A child from a lower socioeconomic stratum may face difficulties in school because he has learned a different set of values than those followed by school personnel and, perhaps, by the majority of the pupils. Because of his home training, he may feel no guilt or shame at wiping his nose on his arm, ignoring homework, and pulling girls into the bushes for physical examinations. Since his value system differs from that of another social-class level, if he wishes to rise in the socioeconomic world he may look forward to conflicts with members of the higher level unless he changes some of his standards.

Superego and needs: Some children develop values that seem incompatible with their own needs. Their standards are too strict for their own mental health. Frequently these standards relate to sexual behavior, to the expression of aggressive feelings, or to intellectual or socioeconomic attainments.

Often parents either imply or directly teach children that sexual drives are shameful evidences of a devil within the individual's soul, even though it is rather easily demonstrated that the sex drive is an expected, persistent, normal component of human personality. The child who grows up to believe sex needs are abnormal and wicked has a built-in maladjustment. Each time normal urges arise, he feels guilt and unworthiness. Another child constantly will be emotionally disturbed when normal feelings of anger and aggression arise within him when he is frustrated, because his parents and teachers have taught him that he should esteem and appreciate other people under all circumstances. Hate and anger, he has been told, are sinful, so his superego tells him of his sin each time hate and anger arise.

The question may then be asked: How can a person's sexual and aggressive drives be controlled if he is not taught that they are bad? The answer is that the conscience can be built to regard these feelings as normal but to recognize that there are both wise

nd unwise ways to express such feelings. Thus when these emo-
ional states arise he need not feel unworthy or abnormal. Instead,
\e learns to accept them, noting at the same time that his society
\as placed certain limits on their expression and that he pays a
rice if he disregards the limits. We conclude, therefore, that
he child who has an unrealistic, overly strict conscience which
unishes him for normal emotions may expect constant maladjust-
nent. On the other hand, the child is less likely to face unneces-
ary maladjustment in meeting society's demands if he recognizes
hat his emotions are universal ones but that society has set up
\imits for their expression.

How, then, do teachers observe the contents of a student's
\uperego—his ideals and his conscience? As in the case of inner
\eeds, this must be a guess or estimate based upon observations
\f what the student says and does. There are two types of students
\hat usually warrant the teacher's attention: those with unduly
\trict or punitive consciences and those with unduly lax ones. We
\hall inspect each of these types in more detail.

Pupils who hold too strict standards for themselves face two
\ossibilities for maladjustment: (1) the inner torture of guilt and
\hame occasioned by acts or thoughts that most of us would con-
\ider normal and (2) conflicts with other people who hold dif-
\erent standards.

(1) Pupils who suffer undue guilt often reveal themselves
\hrough their self-castigation and self-derogation. When they fail
\t a task or make a mistake they may say, "I'm no good" or "I
\ever do anything right." They may break into tears or sulk or
\ound themselves on the head. They may inflict self-punishment
\y denying themselves lunch or an activity they would enjoy. In
\ther instances the strict superego causes the individual to be
\verly shy or fearful. It causes him to be a chronic apologizer or
\o be painfully cautious so that he will not displease anyone or
\will not disagree with anyone. He may worry at length over past
\errors. This kind of pupil usually is not a discipline problem.
Rather, he is typically most obedient, so he is convenient for the
\teacher to have in class. But from the standpoint of the student's
\own psychological growth, he would be better off to stand against
\others on occasion and not be so servile and cringing.

(2) A student who holds strict standards of behavior may be

intolerant of others' standards, and thus he may come into confli
with them. If he considers that swearing is evil or in bad tast
he may express his disgust at the language of classmates or ma
report them to the teacher. When pupils from several social-cla
levels or several religious groups attend the same school, the
may have value conflicts regarding boy-girl relations, propert
rights, speech habits, tolerance for deviant viewpoints, religior
convictions, smoking and drinking, forms of recreation, ways of
settling arguments, and attitudes toward authority.

From the teacher's standpoint, pupils with unduly lax cor
sciences—or at least with standards different from the teacher's—
are the troublemakers. They violate school rules and patterns of
behavior which the school authorities consider proper and polite
Such students do not simply infringe on others' rights or brea
the rules once or twice, but because their consciences operate ac
cording to a different set of values, they continue to violate th
teacher's expectations and apparently feel no guilt or shame. The
do not regret having broken the rules. They only regret havin
been caught at it.

In summary, if a student's inner standards are so strict that h
frequently fails to live up to them, he can expect constant feeling
of guilt and shame. These feelings will show up through his shy
apologetic, or self-castigating behavior. If his standards, on th
other hand, are quite lax or are markedly different from thos
of the school authorities and other students, he can expect th
kinds of problems which occur when an individual is in frequen
conflict with his environment. His behavior will be antisocial o
crude, in the teacher's eyes. In both of these instances the pup
is considered maladjusted because his superego does not fit th
requirements of either his own needs or the outside world.

Nature of the Ego

The ego, as described earlier, is the function of personality tha
assesses the inner needs, the environment, and the superego, the
determines which adjustment techniques will best satisfy all thre
of these varieties of demands. A person's ego is considered stron
and healthy when it consists of an accurate estimate of inne

needs, of personal abilities, and of the demands and opportunities of the environment and superego. In other words, the ego's mental map should correctly represent both the inner life and the outer world.

A teacher typically bases his judgment of the adequacy of a pupil's ego on observations of the adjustment mechanisms the pupil uses and of the way these mechanisms fit the pupil's style of life. After an extended series of observations of a student, the instructor should be able to draw such tentative conclusions as the following:

Ben seldom takes the responsibility for mistakes he makes, either mistakes in schoolwork or in social relations. He almost always rationalizes and offers excuses. By so often blaming others for his own errors, he has managed to alienate most of his classmates. Since he is forever excusing his own behavior, he sees no need to learn to correct mistakes and thus avoid making the same ones in the future. He is due for a good deal of unhappiness if he doesn't readjust his view of himself in relation to others.

Retreat is Katherine's principal reaction to strangers, to new activities, and to difficult problems. She seems to operate on the belief that if nothing is ventured, nothing can be lost. When called upon to answer a question in class, she does not speak but simply sits, red-faced and her head down. If the arithmetic assignment is difficult, she turns to a storybook. If the homework assignment is difficult, she lets it go and tells her mother she is ill so she can stay home when it is due to be handed in. This pattern of behavior forebodes a most unhappy future for Katherine.

In each of his classes Howard is an excellent student. He is well prepared, responsive, and critical. In school and at home his life seems to consist almost entirely of books and of science and art projects. The other students call him "The Grind" and have nothing to do with him socially, though they obviously respect his opinion in class on matters academic. Whether he misses an active social life and companions, I can't tell. Perhaps he finds sufficient companionship in books and in his projects. Perhaps this is a suitable style of life for a boy of his type. Perhaps not.

When Kit first entered my class, she immediately endeared herself to most of her classmates as well as to me. She is pretty, she smiles, and she offers compliments and pleasant banter to everyone. She asks about the interests and opinions of adults to whom she talks. The other teachers who have met her have been equally delighted. But as the semester has progressed, I have come to question the sincerity of Kit's approach. I find that she often is manipulating me and others with sweetness. I believe she sees the world as a place which is best directed for your own uses through elaborate compliments, whether the compliments are deserved or not. This has made me cautious and suspicious of her friendship. Perhaps she would gain more in the long run by being somewhat less effusive.

Barry seems to see the world as a battlefield. He is on one side, and the rest of us are on the other. He expects everyone to be operating contrary to his welfare. Social-studies and English assignments are things to be challenged or disregarded. Remarks by other students are to be sneered at. Displays of friendship are to be suspected. The way he ridicules my attempts to aid him raises my hackles so that I find it difficult to be patient with him. He appears to affect most people this way. Since he expects belligerency from the world, he tends to receive what he expects. Unless he can change his ideas of reality so as to distinguish between friend and foe, his life will become an endless series of conflicts with others.

As the foregoing excerpts suggest, a teacher's observations of students' adjustment techniques enable him to estimate how each student apparently views his own abilities and the world and to predict what the individual's future may be like if he or she continues in the present pattern of behavior. In the examples above, the teacher foresaw adjustment difficulties of a marked nature in the future of Ben, Katherine, and Barry. For Kit only a minor problem was apparent. Howard, the dedicated scholar, was somewhat isolated socially, but on the basis of present evidence it is not clear whether this should be considered a real problem; possibly Howard was launching on a life that would fulfill his needs and also make him a welcome member of society.

How Should Observations Be Collected?

Throughout the preceding discussion we have noted the kinds of behavior which teachers may profitably observe in judging pupil adjustment, but we have not yet discussed the ways that the observations may be most efficiently collected.

Most observations which a teacher makes are informal, unsystematic, and unrecorded. He simply keeps in mind the things he has noticed pupils do during the routine of his day's teaching. His mental notes about a student accumulate throughout the semester to produce an impression of how well the student is fulfilling the expectations of the school. Although such casual, unrecorded classroom observations are of considerable value, they do have several obvious disadvantages. Since the teacher sees only a limited sample of the adjustments the pupil makes to life—a sample typical only in the classroom and on the playground—the teacher may be basing his conclusions on an inaccurate picture of the student's techniques of getting along in his world. In addition, unrecorded observations are frequently forgotten, or else the memory of them may become distorted with time.

Therefore, if the instructor can write down observations he makes—that is, write anecdotal records—and place them in a folder, he will enhance the accuracy of his recall when he later reviews the child's progress toward good adjustment. An accumulation of such notes enables the instructor to make a better balanced assessment of the pupil than if the teacher has depended solely on his memory of incidents.

Another device for recording observations is the rating scale. Rating scales which list the principal forms of behavior that interest the teacher have two advantages. The items on the scale focus the instructor's attention on the types of student actions that he believes are significant. In addition, the scale enables the instructor to systematize his recording of data as he takes time

PERSONAL-SOCIAL ADJUSTMENT SCALE

Student_____ Rater_____ Date_____

| Directions: To summarize your observations of the following aspects of adjustment, check the point on each line that best represents the individual. Comments to clarify any rating may be written on the back of this sheet. | (Check here if not enough evidence for rating.) |

Is he openly friendly toward large numbers of age-mates?

Never   Seldom   Often   Always   _____

Is he friendly toward only one or a few of his age-mates?

Never   Seldom   Often   Always   _____

Is he welcomed into activities by many of his age-mates?

Never   Seldom   Often   Always   _____

Is he antagonistic toward people in authority?

Never   Seldom   Often   Always   _____

Does he follow school and classroom regulations faithfully?

Never   Seldom   Often   Always   _____

Does he accept responsibility for mistakes he makes?

Never   Seldom   Often   Always   _____

Does he complete school assignments willingly and on time?

Never   Seldom   Often   Always   _____

Does he willingly take part in classroom discussion?

Never   Seldom   Often   Always   _____

Does he approach academic tasks with vigor and confidence?

Never   Seldom   Often   Always   _____

Will he vigorously defend his own opinions among his age-mates?

Never   Seldom   Often   Always   _____

periodically to recall each pupil's actions during recent weeks and to summarize his casual observations by checking each pupil's behavior on a scale. The rating sheet developed by one teacher for summarizing casual observations is illustrated above.

OBSERVATIONS BY OTHER PEOPLE

Part of the information about a pupil's adjustment is obtained from comments made by other teachers, by parents, and by other pupils. In utilizing this information, there are two types of caution that an instructor can profitably observe. One relates to the range of behavior that the observer has seen. The other relates to the personal opinions of the observer that may find their way into his report.

The impressions that other people receive about a pupil often reflect only one facet of his life. A mathematics teacher can comment knowledgeably on the pupil's performance in mathematics but not on his performance in art, music, or industrial-arts classes nor on his behavior at home, on the ball field, or at church. Parents are able to comment on the adolescent's relations within the home but may know little of his relationships with boys and girls at school. Therefore, when a teacher secures other people's observations of a student, it is well for him to inquire about the setting in which the observations were derived so as to make clear what facet of the student's overall adjustment has been under surveillance.

Comments written by teachers of previous years are often placed in the student's cumulative-record folders and are passed on to the instructor of the next higher grade. In addition, oral observations are passed from teacher to teacher during lunch hour, recess, or faculty conference periods. Parents and other pupils also serve as informants. Some of these individuals, however, are not careful about limiting their remarks to objective descriptions of pupil behavior. Instead, they insert—often inadvertently—personal opinions into their reports. Such opinions may direct the listener to an inaccurate conclusion. The two most common errors made by informants are the inclusion of *interpretive* and *evaluative* statements in what is purportedly an objective observation.

An interpretive comment implies or states the reason or motive behind the act, such as "*Because* he was tired, John failed to finish his term paper" or "Carol's belief that she is too fat *causes* her to avoid all of the school social events." In each of these cases the observer's estimate of the motive may be accurate, but on the other hand it may be in error. Therefore, the reader of the anecdotal record should keep in mind that the interpretation portion of these statements represents the observer's opinion rather than fact. Other interpretations of this same behavior might have been as reasonable.

An evaluative statement implies or explicitly judges whether the behavior was good or bad, desirable or undesirable. For example, in the written comment, "Fred lured his two naive companions into the test-mark-altering plot," the terms *lure, naive,* and *plot* imply that Fred was malicious, his act was evil, and his companions were not to blame for what happened. Although these implications may actually be correct, it is also possible that if the incident had been reported more objectively and in more detail, the reader of the record might have arrived at a somewhat different conclusion about the boys. For instance, the objective description of this incident should have been:

> When I returned to the classroom after lunch, I saw Fred, Darrell, and Scott come out the rear door and run down the hall to the north exit. Entering the room, I opened the center drawer of my desk to put my purse away and noticed that my grade book was in the front of the drawer rather than in the back where I usually place it. I glanced through the book and discovered that some of the math grades had been altered. After school I located the three boys and interviewed them one at a time. Fred said he knew nothing about the grade book. He said he only came to the room after lunch to sharpen a pencil. Darrell admitted that they had changed marks in the book but denied doing it himself. He said Fred had talked him and Scott into looking at the book "for fun," but that while they looked Fred had changed their test marks to higher ones. Scott said he did nothing in the room. When I asked if Fred had opened the book and had changed test marks, Scott said yes.

The foregoing type of evidence might warrant several interpretations other than the one the teacher gave in her statement about

Fred's luring naïve boys into a plot. It is possible that Darrell had lied and that Scott had said "yes" simply to avoid incriminating himself. Fred's part in the scheme is not at all clear. Hence, such evaluative statements should be regarded with some suspicion unless other information is available to support them.

The terms that some observers include in reports may carry both interpretive and evaluative implications, such as *lazy, poor attitude, ambitious scheming,* or *malicious intent.* When these comments are offered orally, the listener may deem it appropriate to ask the informant for a more specific description of the incident so that the propriety of the use of such terms can be better judged.

PERSONALITY TESTS

Although it is not the teacher's role to administer and interpret personality tests, he should know something about their nature and worth. Certain students in his class may have been studied by a school psychologist so that summaries of the test results appear in the student's file. Furthermore, when the school staff conducts a case study of a student who faces major social-psychological problems, the teacher is properly a participant in case conferences during which personality test results are discussed. Therefore, we shall look briefly at some of the characteristics of the more common personality measuring devices.

A common method of categorizing personality tests is to divide them into *adjustment inventories* and *projective techniques.*

An adjustment inventory is a self-rating scale or questionnaire that consists of a series of statements or questions which a student answers about himself. The statements, ranging in number from fifty to several hundred, are frequently of the following variety:

1. Are you awakened by disturbing dreams?
2. Do you have headaches?
3. Does your mother like you better than your father likes you?
4. Do people treat you unfairly?
5. Are your ambitions higher than you can ever reach?
6. When you make a mistake are you afraid to admit it to other people?
7. Do you feel that most people are not as worried as you are?

8. Do you find more hate in the world than love and friendliness?
9. Do you think things will be much better in the future?
10. Do you like to volunteer answers in class?

Some inventories ask the respondent to mark each of these items *yes* or *no* or *don't know*. Others provide for a series of answers that allow a greater range of opinion, such as *always, often, sometimes, seldom,* and *never.*

When a clinical psychologist interprets a student's answers on an inventory, he tries to see a patterning of responses which shows the nature of the individual's inner life. In other words, he looks for a pattern of the student's needs-system, ego, and superego. However, the interpretation may be faulty because of the limitations that inventories possess as sole measures of personality. One limitation is that an astute student who does not wish to reveal his psychological problems can often predict what a well-adjusted answer to an item should be, so he gives a well-adjusted student's answer rather than his own true one. Second, the items on a particular inventory may not touch upon the facet of life in which the student's disturbance is most pronounced. If he is disturbed about relations with girls, then items about his health, vocational plans, and family ties may not elicit responses which reveal his problem. Third, one student may interpret the words in the inventory differently than does another student or the clinician. If an item asks, "Do you often feel depressed?", the student does not know whether *often* refers to one hour a day or to one hour a week or to almost constant feelings of unhappiness over a period of a year.

Because of their shortcomings, personality inventories cannot serve as secure bases for a comprehensive understanding of a student's personal-social adjustment. At best, they supplement other types of evidence about the individual.

The term *projective techniques* refers to a diversity of stimuli which encourage an individual to reveal, often without his realizing it, certain aspects of his inner life that are not readily illuminated by direct interviews, questionnaires, or short-term observations. The best known projective device is the Rorschach inkblot test. A respondent is asked to look at each of the ten blots in turn and tell what it looks like to him. In this way the student projects from his mind an interpretation of the blots and, hopefully, reveals the viewpoint from which he approaches life. Sometimes, in addition to using inkblots, the psychologist may ask the individual to look at a series of pictures and to make up a story which each picture might illustrate.

In other cases the stimulus for the projection of the respondent's mental map will be a series of incomplete sentences, each of which the student completes as he likes. The following sentence fragments illustrate this type of device:

My mother _____
I'm afraid when _____
Girls are _____
I like to _____
Boys need _____
I wish my father _____
What worries me most is _____

The dozen or two other projective devices in rather common use include incomplete stories, lists of words with which the respondent associates other words, cartoons for which the respondent supplies the captions, pictures of a family of dogs whose thoughts the respondent describes, pictures which the pupil is to draw, dolls and toys the child is to play with, and designs he copies.

Because each person has a somewhat individualistic way of viewing life, the results of projective tests are difficult to interpret. The clinician does not have a securely established set of standards against which to match a student's projective-test responses. Thus the psychologist should try to surmise what view of the world and of self underlies a given student's pattern of answers, but the psychologist should not depend upon projective techniques alone for assessing personality. Rather, the careful clinician uses these results to supplement the evidence he has derived from observations, interviews, self-reports, past records of behavior, medical examinations, and other tests.

Summary

By observing students in the classroom and in extra-class activities, teachers are able to make estimates about how well individuals are fulfilling their own needs and at the same time adjusting to the society in which they live. The teacher's observations are often supplemented by comments received from other teachers, from pupils, and from parents. Most teachers gather their observations in a casual, unsystematic, unrecorded fashion. A smaller percentage, and these usually at the elementary-school level, systematically collect evidence on all pupils' personal-social adjustment, and they record this evidence as anecdotal records or as marks on rating scales. The occasional pupil who has unusually difficult problems may be studied intensively by a team composed of the teacher, a psychologist or counselor, the school nurse, the principal, and a social worker. The data about the pupil are collected in the form of a case study so that wise steps may be taken toward correcting the pupil's problem.

CHAPTER 7

INDIVIDUALITY VERSUS MALADJUSTMENT

Both sociologists and educators in recent years have assailed the forces in society which would cast each person into the same mold of thought and action, allowing little opportunity for the individual to develop his unique style of life. If a teacher is seriously concerned about this danger of standardization, and if he wishes to encourage a healthy amount of individuality in students, he must face two questions before he attempts to alter their thoughts and actions:

What types and degrees of deviant behavior should be tolerated or encouraged because they represent an individual's style of life?

What types and degrees should a teacher try to change because they are symptoms of personal-social maladjustment?

Although there is no one answer which is applicable to all students, there are several questions which a teacher can ask himself in order to arrive at a decision about individual cases he meets. These questions include:

1. Is the student's behavior considered odd by one segment of society (such as the teacher's own social-class or religious group) but regarded as natural by another segment in which the student seeks acceptance and respect? If a high-school boy from a lower socioeconomic level appears in school with a mustache and sideburns, and from all indications he does not yearn to achieve middle-class status, there appears to be no good reason for the teacher to urge removal of the mustache or to make fun of the boy, despite the fact that such adornment among adolescents is considered inappropriate within middle-class society. On the other hand, when a fifth-grade girl weeps at the least criticism by her age-mates or her teacher, she needs help in developing more adequate methods of adjusting to frustration, because frequent crying on the part of ten-year-olds is not considered a desirable characteristic in any segment of society.

2. *Does the behavior harm others or violate their rights?* In certain subcultures of American society it is rather normal for youths to carry switchblades and to fight with rocks and bricks. Despite the normality (in the sense of being commonplace) of these acts, the school cannot tolerate them because they are likely to harm others. Furthermore, teachers are warranted in trying to change the behavior of students who harm classmates psychologically through taunting them for their physical handicaps (lameness, nearsightedness) or social handicaps (divorced parents, membership in a minority group), religious practices or intellectual shortcomings. On the other hand, a girl who wishes to spend most of her free time by herself reading or drawing is not interfering with other people's rights and thus should be allowed to pursue her activities unmolested by the teacher's efforts to socialize her, if the girl's needs seem adequately satisfied.

3. *Is the behavior symptomatic of unfulfilled needs, of fears, or of inadequate social techniques on the student's part?* Observational techniques like those described in Chapter 6 aid the teacher in judging whether strong unfulfilled needs are the causes for overly aggressive acts which alienate peers whose friendship is really desired, for shyness which prevents the pupil from accomplishing things which would earn him the self-respect he needs, or for constant self-pity which distracts him from analyzing his own shortcomings and doing something to correct them. Such students are not simply exhibiting a healthy individuality which should be encouraged. They need help in understanding themselves and in changing their methods of adjustment.

4. *Is the behavior somewhat unusual for the individual's present age level but more common and desirable among people older than he?* The gifted child, in particular, may act in ways which are atypical for his age level but suitable for older youth. For instance, a sixth-grade boy, exhibiting good logic, may frequently be critical of the patterns of reasoning of his age-mates, his teachers, and the authors of textbooks used at his grade level. Some instructors view such a critical attitude with alarm. They

believe the boy is disturbed because he appears to be antagonistic toward others, particularly toward authority figures "whom he should respect." To force him to comply with more typical sixth-grade behavior, these teachers exert pressure by means of low marks, sarcasm, frowning, and exhortations. However, even though the boy's behavior is not typical of his age level, it is a variety deemed desirable at a later age. Astute critical analysis, expressed in polite terms, is a valued commodity among people of importance in the adult world. Thus the teacher might more properly be expected to encourage politely expressed analysis and criticism rather than to try to squelch it.

Although some teachers may resist such an advanced trait as critical ability, they usually recognize and enthusiastically encourage other kinds of atypical, advanced behavior which do not threaten their own authority or their opinions, such as the gifted child's interests in literature, in play writing, in scientific experimentation, in hobbies like stamp and coin collecting, and in art and music.

It is sometimes difficult to determine whether a gifted child's preoccupation with books or with a hobby represents a true interest or serves instead as a compensation for, or escape from, other responsibilities (school assignments) or unsatisfactory social relations (rejection by schoolmates). However, if the teacher is to decide whether to try to alter the individuality or to encourage it, he must make this decision about whether the engrossing activity is an appropriate interest or an undesirable escape.

Summary

We conclude that teachers should tolerate and/or encourage individuality which fulfills all of the following conditions: does not violate others' rights, is not symptomatic of damaging fears or strong unfulfilled needs, is not simply an escape from reasonable responsibilities, and is suitable within the segment of society by which the individual hopes to be accepted. When teachers apply these criteria in judging the desirability of a student's deviant behavior, they find that heretofore they may have arbitrarily attempted to alter certain kinds of acts simply because they were atypical acts, not because the student really would be better adjusted if he became more *average*. In short, teachers should not simply try to mold students into images of the teachers themselves nor to mold students into an ideal form which would be unsuited to the individual's style of life.

CHAPTER 8

A PROCESS FOR AIDING
THE MALADJUSTED

Before inspecting the case studies which compose Part Three, it seems desirable to review in a concise form the steps which have been suggested in earlier chapters for aiding the maladjusted pupil.

1. The teacher observes students as accurately as possible. He analyzes the adequacy of their behavior from the standpoint of his theory of personality. From the viewpoint of this book, the analysis is intended to indicate how well students are fulfilling their needs, meeting their responsibilities to society, satisfying the demands of their ideals and conscience, and developing an accurate understanding of their world.

2. When the teacher suspects, on the basis of observations, that a given student is not well adjusted, the teacher tries to secure further evidence from the opinions of other people or, in some cases, from an analysis by a psychologist, psychiatrist, or psychiatric social worker. The teacher may also interview the student or observe him in situations intended to reveal the kind of maladjustment that is suspected.

3. If the teacher concludes that the deviant behavior of the student is simply an individualistic style of life and not a real maladjustment, the teacher does not attempt to change the student's personality or environment.

4. If the teacher concludes that a true maladjustment exists, he tries to estimate what feasible measures he might take to reorder the student's perception of life, his adjustment techniques, or his environment. When the maladjustment appears serious, the teacher tries to refer the student to a psychologist, psychiatrist, or clinic for expert diagnosis and treatment. At the same time the teacher tries to use his own tentative diagnosis of the student's

problem as the basis for treating the student more adequately in class. If the student does enter into treatment with a psychologist or psychiatrist, the teacher seeks advice from the therapist concerning what classroom measures would best aid the pupil.

5. When the maladjustment does not appear to be a major one, or when it is serious but no therapeutic help is available, the teacher must rely on his own analysis of the problem as a basis for classroom treatment.

6. As the instructor determines what steps he will take to aid the pupil, he keeps in mind the distinctions between his own role and that of the clinician. That is, the teacher does not set for himself goals of personality reordering as ambitious as would typically be set by a clinician.

7. In designing classroom approaches for aiding the disturbed pupil, the teacher is never sure that the measures he intends to try will work effectively in this case. Rather, on the basis of his knowledge of past cases of students who seemed similar to the one now faced, the instructor tries out measures which he believes might work. That is, each new pupil is somewhat unique and thus represents a new experiment for the teacher or therapist.

8. When an attempted treatment is not effective, the teacher recognizes that his original estimate or hypothesis of what the student needed was somewhat in error, so he tries to correct his earlier estimate and approach the student in another manner. In short, the treatment process becomes a pattern of approximating a solution, then correcting the shortcomings of it if it has not worked satisfactorily. As the cases in Part Three illustrate, there is no set of proven recipes for proper treatments which can apply to all students. Rather, the teacher uses his general understanding of people—his theory of personality—as the basis for designing whatever aid he thinks might be feasible in the classroom for satisfying the shortcomings in the student's personality or environment. The following cases suggest the variety of kinds of aid that are possible in actual classroom situations at elementary- and secondary-school levels.

Part Three

CLASSROOM CASES OF MALADJUSTMENT

I t is the writer's conviction that teachers often gain their greatest insights into ways to aid disturbed students if they can participate vicariously—by means of motion pictures or written case studies—in the process of working with specific children. For this reason the following twenty-one cases are presented, each with an introductory note which is intended to emphasize some aspect of that case which deserves particular attention.

The presentation of each case follows the same four-step pattern:

1. The student's problem situation is described.
2. The teacher's estimate of the factors causing the problem is outlined.
3. The teacher's treatment of the student is explained.
4. The apparent success of the treatment is noted.

For each of the four grade-level divisions (primary, intermediate, junior high, senior high) several cases are analyzed.

CHAPTER 9

FIVE CASES IN PRIMARY GRADES

The following examples illustrate ways teachers helped children in kindergarten through third grade.

CASE I: FEARS AND READING DIFFICULTIES

If a child-guidance clinic is available in the community, the teacher may refer the markedly disturbed child and his parents to the clinic for aid. The teacher's responsibility thereafter becomes one of cooperating with the therapist in carrying out the school phase of the treatment program while the major burden for diagnosis and treatment lies with the clinician. This pattern was followed in the case of Tommy Nolan.[1]

The Precipitating Problem

After a moderately successful year in first grade, Tommy began in the first two months of second grade to exhibit difficulties with reading and arithmetic. In addition, he often seemed afraid to go to school, he was reluctant to play with other children, and he tended to break into tears. These were behaviors he had not shown since his early kindergarten days. The second-grade teacher, who also had taught Tommy in first grade, suggested to Tommy's mother the third month of school that she take the boy to the child-guidance clinic for aid.

Causal Factors and Treatment

The teacher was puzzled about the boy's fears and crying, and she did not understand the basis for his increasing difficulties with reading and arithmetic. She suspected that he might be develop-

[1] Helen Leland Witmer (ed.). *Psychiatric Interviews with Children.* New York: The Commonwealth Fund, 1946, pp. 59–92.

ing a neurosis or that something about his home life was affecting him. But since she did not have the time or training to conduct an accurate diagnosis, she referred him to the clinician.

Tommy came to the clinic one hour a week for five months. During each session he worked with the clinical psychologist in a playroom (equipped with toys and easels and a blackboard) while his mother talked with a social worker in another part of the building. During the first session Tommy was shy and fearful. But he soon recognized that the psychologist liked him, that she accepted his ideas without criticism, and that she was greatly impressed with his drawing skill. In the first two sessions the therapist did not press the boy to face the principal reasons he was coming to the clinic: difficulties with schoolwork. But Tommy soon was able to bring up this issue himself. As he sought the psychologist's help with his current week's spelling words, the clinician discovered that the boy's unusually acute photographic memory (his eidetic imagery), which accounted for his accuracy in drawing, was at the center of his difficulties with reading and spelling. That is, Tommy did not recognize the connection between the sight of a word and its sound. He had stumbled through first grade by memorizing words and pages of sentences by sight without knowing their meanings. In spelling he had memorized the word list by sight, then had written the list in the same order. With the therapist's guidance, Tommy now came to recognize—and with considerable amazement and pleasure—the relationships among spoken and written words. This information about the cause of the boy's reading difficulties was transmitted to the school so that the teacher could henceforth design special reading instruction which furthered Tommy's phonics skills.

Although his schoolwork improved, Tommy still remained fearful, so his mother continued to bring him to the clinic. As the social worker talked with her and as Tommy expressed himself through creating dramas with dolls representing a family, a nonscholastic basis for the boy's fears became evident. That is, his mother's resentment toward the father for his lack of steady employment was not vented on the father but was redirected toward Tommy through such acts as frequent scolding, insistence that he stay in after school to study, and criticism of his desire to draw.

As the mother talked with the social worker and as Tommy worked with the psychologist, they came to recognize the causes for the tensions within the family, and as a result they began to understand each other better and to resolve their antagonisms. In short, by readjusting their mental maps of the family relationship, Tommy and his mother could understand each other's motives and needs so as to develop a more compatible family life.

Success of Treatment

By the end of the five months of weekly sessions, Tommy had caught up with his average classmates in reading, arithmetic, and spelling so that he could progress satisfactorily without the remedial reading sessions he had needed at the beginning of the school year. His mother recognized that Tommy needed to play with other children after school, and she discussed with her husband her concern over his unemployment rather than suppressing her disturbed feelings and taking them out on Tommy. The boy also recognized now that the anger which his parents sometimes vented toward him was not his fault but was a result of their being tired and worried over other matters. At the end of the therapeutic sessions Tommy was a boy who liked school, enjoyed his parents more, and did not show the fears or the tendency to cry which he had exhibited when he had first entered the clinic.

Because Tommy recovered rapidly from his disturbance, it is apparent that he was not a child suffering from a deep neurosis. Rather, he was in a period of temporary maladjustment occasioned by a combination of lack of success in school (because of an inaccurate understanding of the nature of written language) and a disordered home life (because of parental conflict that was caused by the local economic depression). Many problem cases treated in clinics are not so readily resolved as this one.

CASE II: RAGE

The case of Mary Romano shows one teacher's strategy in working with (1) a girl who shattered the calm of classrooms with her rage and (2) a mother who spurned the suggestion that her daughter's behavior was not typical.

The Problem Situation

Mary's family moved in late December from the east side to
the west side of a small Western city. In January, Mary first
entered the third grade of Westside School. Before the girl's
arrival, the city's guidance department in late December had
forwarded a thick file testifying that Mary had been one of the
prime social-psychological problems for the staff of Eastside School.
From kindergarten into third grade she had dismayed teachers
and classmates alike by exploding when things failed to go her
way. If frustrated, she would yell, pound her head, and finish by
sobbing disconsolately. The Eastside staff was not sorry to see her
leave.

The third-grade teacher in Westside School, forewarned by this
record of emotional outbursts, awaited Mary with misgivings.
When the girl entered her new classroom, it was clear to both
teacher and pupils that she was different. Her blue skirt was much
longer than that of any other girl. Her straggly, matted hair suggested that it had not been combed for days. She looked like a
child with problems at home as well as at school.

An Estimate of Underlying Cause

From reading the file of information on the girl, the teacher
learned that Mary was an only child whose parents both worked.
In her early years Mary had been brought up primarily by her
maternal grandmother. When her parents had been invited during the past year to talk with her teachers and the school psychologist about her explosive behavior, her mother had bitterly
criticized the school staff as meddlers and the father had ignored
the request for a conference. In view of these negative reactions
to school personnel, the third-grade teacher in Mary's new school
decided not to contact the parents for a month or two. She hoped
they would "cool off," and she wished to make her own observations of the girl's conduct before talking with them.

The records from Eastside School indicated that Mary's academic ability was at least adequate but her motor coordination
was poor.

Her new teacher decided that her initial strategy would be: (1) to welcome Mary warmly and to encourage the other children to adopt a similar friendly attitude, (2) to explain the classroom rules clearly and be firm in seeing that Mary observed them, and (3) because of the girl's apparent motor-coordination problems, to accept without criticism written work that was not particularly neat and playground behavior that was not very agile.

Method of Treatment

On Mary's first day in school the teacher told the class:

I'm happy to introduce Mary Romano, your new classmate. Mary, we're glad to have you with us. I know it's hard to move into a new school in the middle of the year, because you have to get used to new people and different ways of doing things. But we'll help you all we can. Early last fall these boys and girls and I talked about how we might conduct our class so we would all get along well together. The chart on the side wall shows some of the rules we agreed on. We also have some others that we'll explain from time to time.

Whenever a new girl comes, we assign her a special classmate to introduce her to the school. We've asked Joanne to be your special helper. But feel free to ask anyone else for aid also. We're all glad to help. Now, the first thing to decide is where you'll sit. As you see, we have four empty desks. You may choose any of them you like.

This choice proved to be Mary's first problem. In a loud, belligerent voice she announced that she would not sit beside a boy. It took ten minutes to arrive at a satisfactory solution. As the morning progressed she displayed a habit which was to disturb the class the rest of the year—shouting forth her opinions whether someone else was talking at the time or not.

During recess and lunch the other girls made sincere overtures of friendship. Mary hardly reacted to them at all.

On the third day of class, as Mary walked down the aisle to sharpen her pencil, she hit each child on the head as she passed, apparently to attract attention. The teacher took her aside and told her in friendly but firm tones, "I'm afraid you don't understand, Mary. We don't do that in this class." Mary looked at the teacher carefully, then answered, "All right," and the incident was never repeated.

During the first week, as the teacher explained some arithmetic problems to Mary, she put her arm around the girl's shoulder. Mary drew away quickly and asked, "Why did you do that?" The teacher said, "I like you boys and girls. That's why I sometimes touch you, just as friends often do." Mary said, "I don't like it. I don't like people to touch me."

Throughout the following weeks she proved to be an increasingly diligent, able student. Though she continued to shout out in class in an uncontrolled manner and often complained when not permitted to do things just her own way, she never broke into a rage.

After two months the teacher mailed the following letter to Mary's home:

> Mary is doing beautiful work in school, especially in reading. But she does have some trouble adjusting to the other children. I feel that she needs help in getting along with others. If you could arrange to come to school some day to talk with me, perhaps you could suggest some things we might do to aid her.

When the teacher received no reply, she asked Mary if her mother had received the letter. Mary said, "Yes. She was awfully mad."

Two weeks later when the teacher phoned each child's parents to invite them to an open-house evening, she asked Mrs. Romano whether they might meet some day and talk. Mrs. Romano said she could not come to school because she worked every day. The teacher said that she herself would come to the Romano home some evening if Mrs. Romano did not object. The mother agreed.

When the teacher appeared for the visit, Mrs. Romano's first words were:

> I just want you to know I'm not buying any of this. I know what you school people are up to. At Eastside they tried to blame me. They don't have to tell me how to run my family. I'm not buying any of it.

The teacher told her:

It's difficult for me to come here to tell you that your child is not satisfactory. I thought about it a long while before I came. I knew it might be futile, but I decided I would try, because I like Mary and I want her to be happy and successful. If she is helped now, perhaps she can work it out all right. But if she is not, I'm afraid for her future. I thought that you and I between us might work out a plan to help her.

Then the teacher told Mrs. Romano an incident in her own life which involved a medical doctor telling her some things she did not want to hear and she had become angry. The incident, which had a comical ending, caused the mother to laugh with the teacher, and tension which originally had existed between them was relaxed. Mrs. Romano was able to talk about her daughter without being so defensive. She described Mary's childhood and the influence of her grandmother, whom Mrs. Romano pictured as a forceful, domineering woman with a will of iron. "Mary's a lot like her," she said.

The teacher told Mrs. Romano that Mary was doing fine academic work, and the mother said, "This is the first time she's learned anything in school. They didn't teach her anything at Eastside." This remark, in light of the fact that Mary had already been a good reader when she had entered the new classroom, suggested that Mrs. Romano had never before really known how the girl was succeeding in schoolwork.

In discussing the girl's problems of shouting out in class and being brusque with the other children, the teacher explained that she believed Mary needed compliments and encouragement but also fair and firm rules that gave her a sense of order and a trustworthy environment. The teacher indicated that Mary had not had one of her customary temper tantrums in the new school. Mrs. Romano said she would do whatever she could to help see that Mary continued to succeed in school. Although the teacher was pleased by this new conciliatory attitude on the mother's part, she did not expect any basic changes in the personal relations in the home which had apparently caused Mary to adopt her current style of life. The most the teacher expected was to have the parents tell the girl that they were happy with her successes in school and to have them support whatever suggestions the teacher might make in the future to aid the girl.

Three weeks later at school Mary came to class in an unusually irritable mood. She sniffled and sneezed; the teacher surmised that she was catching a cold so that her tolerance for frustration was lower than usual. She took Mary to the school nurse's office to lie down. But before an hour had passed, the nurse called the teacher on the interclassroom communication system: "Come quick. We're having a tizzy." When the teacher arrived, she found Mary sobbing. It was the final stage of one of the girl's traditional fits of rage. Just before the tantrum, the girl had shouted, "I can't stand to stay here. I want to go back to class." When the nurse had told her to lie down quietly, the screaming and head pounding had begun. The teacher now told Mary, "It's almost lunchtime. So dry your tears, wash your face, and eat. You come back with us after lunch."

At the end of the semester the teacher summarized the technique which she had found to be successful with Mary.

> I treat her as much as possible like everyone else. Although I still try to encourage her to hold up her hand rather than to shout out when she wants to express her opinion, I don't press her too hard on this point. I can usually tell when she is building up more tension than she can retain, and I arrange not to make frustrating demands on her at those times. I think that she gets some sense of security and order if I am kind, fair, and firm.

Success of Treatment

By June, Mary could be credited with four kinds of improvement. Her academic progress was better than it had ever been in her former school, particularly in reading, arithmetic, and spelling. Her social relationships were less than cordial, but they had improved over her first month in school. She had never broken into a rage in the classroom or on the playground. And her shouting aloud in class had become less frequent.

Her basic problem, however, had not been solved. She was still a disturbed girl. Apparently some basic changes in the emotional relationships within her family would be needed before Mary could be expected to improve her own style of life. The teacher had observed that Mary's mother was herself strong-willed and short-tempered. Under these circumstances, significant alterations in the way the girl's family behaved toward her could not be expected. Mary probably would always be a disturbed person. The best the school could do would be to help her succeed in academic work and to learn to live more amicably within society's usual expectations for social behavior.

CASE III: VERBAL IMPOVERISHMENT

Many teachers seem prone to conclude that a pupil who stares dumbly when asked a simple question is stupid and should be in a special class for the mentally deficient. But a variety of causes other than meager intellectual endowment can underlie a child's simpleton appearance. Unless the pupil's unique personality and background are investigated in some detail, the true cause for his unresponsiveness may go undiscovered. And when the cause is unclear, the solution is hard to come by.

The case of J. V. Martin illustrates how a kindergarten teacher worked with a school psychologist to find the apparent source of a small Negro boy's reticence. As a consequence, the teacher and psychologist were able to organize a successful home-school approach to the boy's problem.

The Problem Situation

At first J.V. looked like just another shy kindergarten child who, after a few weeks in school, would emerge from his cloak of timidity and enter into the chatter of the group. But by January he still had hardly talked. And on the occasions when he did speak, he uttered only monosyllabic whispers. The teacher asked the psychologist who worked in the school once a week to study the boy and, along with the teacher, to develop an approach which might help him speak louder and more frequently.

An Estimate of Underlying Cause

The psychologist, in the informal role of social worker, had already visited J.V.'s home in December, three months after the

boy had entered kindergarten. This first visit was not to investigate the boy's speech habits but to determine the general welfare
status of the home. A private welfare agency had heard that there
was currently no father in the Martin household, so that Mrs.
Martin was left alone and unemployed to care for J.V. and three
younger siblings. The psychologist had been asked by the agency
to recommend what type of help Mrs. Martin should be given.

The psychologist found Mrs. Martin to be a shy but friendly
young woman who had moved to this Northern community from
the Deep South during the past summer. In the South the family
had lived in a remote shack on a farm, far from any neighbors.
Now in the North they lived in a humble house in a lower-class
section of the city. The Martin living room was clean but contained only a small couch, a straight chair, and a television set.
The psychologist recommended to the welfare agency that Mrs.
Martin receive assistance.

During January and February the psychologist visited the
kindergarten frequently to become acquainted with J.V. She
chatted with—or mostly *at*—him about pictures in books or about
the animals which sixth graders kept in a nearby room. She often
put her arm around the boy or held his hand to establish a closer
personal bond with him. One day after school while she stood
outside the front entrance, she felt a small hand pressed into her
own, and she looked down into J.V.'s expressionless face. He led
her to the lawn beside the front walk and pointed to a ladybug
which he had spied on a blade of grass. She praised him for his
skill at observation.

On several occasions J.V. willingly accompanied the psychologist to her office to "talk and play some games." The games were
such psychological tests as the Columbia Mental Maturity Scale,
on which J.V. earned an IQ of 84,* and others that required him
to interpret the meaning of pictures. During these individual
sessions J.V. was more communicative, but still he spoke in
whispers. The psychologist kept telling him in a gentle manner,
"I can't quite hear, so you'll have to speak out loud to help me
hear." When thus urged, J.V. would speak above a whisper.

---

* Psychologists generally regard scores between about 90 and 110 to
represent average intellectual performance.

Meanwhile the teacher made her own observations of the boy's behavior to determine whether he seemed mentally retarded or emotionally disturbed. When she gave directions to the children, she noted that J.V. complied without any apparent confusion. Such evidence of ready understanding increased as the months passed and he became more accustomed to school. He liked to look at picture books. He appeared attentive when other children performed in class or told about their experiences during "show and tell" time.

In early February the teacher wrote the following note in the record about the boy:

> He now seems more secure and will try to do projects—most of the time. He now smiles at times and seems to be enjoying activities such as stories and games—mainly where he can watch. To get my attention he comes beside me and pokes me. He might then in a faint whisper tell what he wants, or else I have to guess. For various reasons I've phoned the mother several times. She seems cooperative. Her younger children keep her busy. I'm considering having J.V. kept in kindergarten a second year.

The psychologist's second visit to the home was made in February, specifically to investigate the boy's verbal and intellectual environment. She learned that the mother rarely talked to her children except to summon them or give an order. Mrs. Martin said that in the South, J.V. had never been around other children, except his brother who was one year younger. Even in their new home, the boys played by themselves in their own yard, usually without conversing. Mrs. Martin said, "When I work around the house I sometimes sing to myself, but I'm not the kind that talks much. I never thought of talking to the boys."

As the result of the information they had gathered, the kindergarten teacher and psychologist agreed that J.V.'s reticence seemed to result from an impoverished verbal environment. They believed his academic intelligence was at least normal and maybe higher, because he reacted alertly to happenings about him. Though he was silent, he behaved "intelligently."

The psychologist, in referring to the Columbia Mental Maturity score, said:

> In J.V.'s case, that score probably can't be trusted. From his sterile verbal environment, he hasn't had the chance to learn the names of many objects which other children have known for some time. He doesn't know the names for colors, so he failed items requiring that knowledge.

When the psychologist or teacher asked J.V. about objects in books which they had looked through together at some earlier time, he easily recalled such names as *elephant* and *dinosaur* and could correctly identify pictures of them.

Hence, teacher and psychologist concluded that J.V. did not suffer from mental retardation or a deep emotional constriction, but that he simply was following the silent style of life—the adjustment mechanism of reticence—which his environment had logically guided him into. The school's plan for treating the boy's problem was built upon this estimate of cause.

Method of Treatment

The plan involved three main elements: (1) The provision of a school atmosphere that would help J.V. feel secure, welcome, important, and not threatened or overwhelmed by the multitude of strange stimuli and people he faced at school. (2) Safe opportunities for speaking—opportunities involving little risk of failure. (3) Reasons to speak and rewards for doing so; that is, if the boy was to give up the safety of his current style of life—reticence —he would have to be convinced that changing into a more loquacious child would be more rewarding than holding to his silence.

To carry out the plan, the teacher frequently sat with J.V. sometime during the morning to talk about picture books, about drawing and painting, or about the picture puzzles or blocks he played with. In a gentle manner she asked many questions. Since his answers were always in a whisper, she often said, "A bit louder, please. I didn't quite hear." And he would answer aloud.

During the day when she stood near J.V. as the class played a game or as she read them a story, she frequently touched his arm or shoulder or hugged him with one arm or held his hand a moment. He never retreated from these demonstrations of affection. He appeared to enjoy them.

The teacher had observed in the past that shy children often are able to make their initial public speaking appearances if some device is provided which permits them some psychological distance from a direct confrontation with the fearsome audience composed of their classmates. The device might be a mask, a costume, a puppet, or a mock television set. The teacher tried a puppet with J.V. She first demonstrated how a puppet on her hand could perform and talk. Then she asked some of the more outgoing, bolder children to try it. Later she invited J.V. to take a turn, and he did. Though his puppet spoke only in whispers, it gained a good deal of praise from the teacher.

On other occasions children were invited to stand behind a mock television set that had been constructed from a cardboard box. Each such performer was asked to sing a song he had learned in kindergarten or at home. By late March, J.V. had voluntarily performed in the box. His song was whispered, but he completed it while looking directly out at the audience. The teacher considered this a significant triumph. J.V. had now become sufficiently self-confident to identify himself directly as the performer; he no longer needed the puppet as his disguise. In late April he sang aloud from the television box.

Between February and April the psychologist had visited J.V.'s mother twice to discuss ways she might help the boy overcome his reticence at home. On the first occasion the psychologist had recommended that Mrs. Martin buy some inexpensive storybooks at the supermarket and read them to J.V. She further had advised Mrs. Martin to talk with J.V. and the younger children more often. When the mother had said she would not know what to talk about, the psychologist had suggested:

When you're cooking or working around the house, just say aloud what you're doing, like, "Now we mix the flour and stir it, and we put in some nutmeg and stir it again." It may sound silly to you at first, but it's what the children need in order to get used to hearing more speech and to learn to speak more themselves. You can also talk with J.V. about what he saw and did at school.

More than a month later, when the second visit was made to the Martin home, the psychologist learned that J.V. was talking more freely. His mother had bought seven small books, which J.V. enjoyed looking through. But she said she could not bring herself to read to him very much, because by nighttime she was tired or else she had friends visiting her. She did, however, talk more with the children as she went about her work, and she seemed pleased with the results.

The psychologist, in addition to visiting the home and spending some time with the boy in the kindergarten, periodically took him to her office to chat as he drew pictures or inspected interesting objects that she had brought.

In brief, the attack on J.V.'s speech problem consisted of a cooperative effort among the classroom teacher, the mother, and the psychologist.

Success of Treatment

By June, J.V. still was a quiet boy. At school he usually did not speak unless he was questioned. And though he still tended to talk in whispers, he would now speak aloud when asked to do so. The times that he would offer a comment of his own volition were increasing. He would sing out loud in front of the class, and he was much less hesitant about attempting new tasks. In effect, during the year he had made notable progress toward altering the style of life which had been shaped for him by a verbally barren environment.

CASES IV AND V: IMPAIRED MOTOR SKILLS

Perceptual-motor or neuromuscular activities are those requiring a person to perceive his environment and then react to it physically. That is, he not only thinks about what he has seen or heard or felt, he also makes an overt response to his perception.

Perceptual-motor problems are rather frequently related to the personal-social difficulties suffered by children and youth. In some cases the malfunction of the perceptual-motor system is the principal cause of the personal-social maladjustment. In other cases it seems that the child's apparent lack of coordination is the symptom of a psychological conflict he is suffering rather than the direct result of a faulty perceptual-motor mechanism.

We have used here such qualifying words as "seems" and "apparent" in recognition of the fact that the physiology of the brain and the chemistry of the nervous system as they influence human behavior are still not well understood. But enough is known to indicate that some children's poor coordination is rather directly the result of physical damage to the circuitry of the central nervous system. When physicians have used forceps during difficult births to help draw the baby from the womb, undue pressure on the baby's soft cranium may damage the brain beneath, doing apparently irreparable harm to the brain's ability to function efficiently. Tumors, insufficient blood supply, toxic substances, and such diseases as meningitis can likewise damage neural tissue. If the injury has been to those portions of the brain that coordinate neuromuscular activities, the child unwittingly behaves in uncoordinated ways.

But all poor coordination probably does not arise solely from a damaged nervous system. Clinical studies suggest that some people's ineptitude or clumsiness is really a symptom of personal-social maladjustment. In other words, the clumsiness is an adjustment mechanism which the child or youth has hit upon—usually unconsciously—as a technique for fulfilling some need, or at least as a confused reaction to a problem in his life. Some people who are more prone than average to suffer accidents are people who conceivably feel guilty about some internal conflict in their lives and thus they unconsciously engage in clumsy behavior so that they must suffer the physical pain of an accident. By thus punishing themselves, they are able to alleviate the guilt feelings of the internal conflict. Other people may have found that they have gained sympathy, or at least attention, when they displayed clumsiness, and thereafter they unconsciously have exaggerated the original incoordination so as to enjoy further attention. Or, in still other cases, a child who does perhaps experience some slight neuromuscular confusion during his toddling years and in middle childhood may also suffer at these times some emotional problems arising from his disturbed relations with other people. It is conceivable that the emotional difficulties, coming at a time that the child is trying to master psychomotor skills, will cause him sufficient psychological confusion to arrest or retard his neuromuscular coordination.

In sum, at our present stage of knowledge of perceptual-motor development it appears that incoordination can be caused either by physical damage to the central nervous system, by psychological conflicts within the individual which yield symptoms of poor coordination, or by some combination of physical and psychological causes. Cases IV and V picture two primary-grade children whose motor skills were impaired. The impairment in each of these cases apparently resulted from somewhat different causes.

CASE IV: THE PROBLEM AND ITS CAUSE

Nine-year-old Dorothy McClure's perceptual-motor trouble was explained by her mother when she first registered the girl in second grade. Dorothy suffered from a neuromuscular incoordination caused by cerebral palsy, which in turn was apparently the result of a birth injury.

By definition, cerebral (*brain*) palsy (*paralysis*) is a disorder involving damage to the central nervous system. Among cerebral-palsy victims, the degree of motor disability resulting from malfunction of the brain centers can vary widely. At one end of the scale are those people whose malady is evidenced only by a minor limp or a slight awkwardness in handwriting or a slight thickness of speech. At the other extreme are those whose limbs shake in constant tremors and/or whose speech mechanism is rendered useless by uncontrollable muscle spasms. Dorothy McClure's disability fell toward the less serious end of this scale. Her style of walking was noticeably, though not seriously, awkward. She seldom tried to run; but when she did, she lumbered somewhat precariously. Her handwriting was painfully slow; the words straggled and jerked above and below the guidelines on the note paper. However, her speech mechanism was in good order and she made constant public use of it. In second grade her reading, arithmetic, and listening skills were not problems. In these areas she was well up with her class. But when she faced writing activities she could not make her muscles obey well enough to half finish an assignment by the time all of her classmates had completed it.

Before moving to her present neighborhood at the beginning of second grade, Dorothy had attended a parochial school for two years, both of which were spent in the first grade. Prior to her parochial-school experience she had been in a cerebral-palsy clinic for a year receiving special training in neuromuscular coordination. At the present time she was not sufficiently disabled to be placed in a clinic or special class, but still she was not normal.

In addition to Dorothy's difficulties with handwriting, two other characteristics troubled her teacher. First was the girl's general clumsiness in operating her arms and legs. Second was her tendency to live in a fantasy world much of the time. Dorothy's fantasy world was populated by a variety of characters, human and animal. She talked of, and to, an imaginary husband for whom she kept house and prepared meals. Her favorite animal was a fantasied cat named George. On the playground or during lunchtime, Dorothy carried on a running line of chatter, whether anyone listened or not, and often the chatter was about the antics of the fantastic characters. The teacher was afraid that if Dorothy spent so much time in her dream world, she would increasingly lose contact with the real world or at least would not be able to distinguish clearly between fantasy and reality.

Method of Treatment

The second-grade teacher along with the school's curriculum coordinator estimated that Dorothy needed aid in: (1) demonstrating—preferably in written form—her understanding of the subject matter being studied, (2) improving her ability to control her limbs, (3) gaining recognition for her accomplishments so that she would maintain a high opinion of herself, and (4) distinguishing between the real and the fantastic.

The teacher tried several approaches to help Dorothy complete written assignments despite her laborious handwriting. Sometimes the instructor had the girl report orally the answers to questions on an assignment or on a test. However, such individual treatment was not possible on most assignments because the teacher needed to devote the major portion of her time to the entire class. The teacher also worked directly on the girl's handwriting by providing unlined paper so that Dorothy would not become so tense trying to keep the letters on the guidelines. (Tension further impairs the cerebral-palsy victim's ability to coordinate eye with hand.) Dorothy's mother agreed to help by supervising her daughter in completing written work at home when the girl was unable to finish it at school. Occasionally Dorothy was given a classmate as a secretary to write down ideas that Dorothy dictated in fulfilling a written assignment. The teacher suggested to the school psychologist that Dorothy be taught how to use a tape recorder as a substitute for written assignments, but the psychologist recommended they turn to the recorder only as a last resort; he wanted Dorothy to work diligently on her writing skills to improve them, rather than have her view the tape recorder as a convenient escape from learning to write more adequately.

In trying to aid Dorothy with controlling her gross body movements more skillfully, the school's part-time physical-education instructor conducted a series of special lessons to teach exercises to children who lacked satisfactory perceptual-motor coordination. The instructor's background in physiotherapy enabled him to design activities suited to alleviating the disabilities of the individuals in the group. In working with Dorothy, he found that oftentimes she would not even attempt a given exercise. She would excuse herself with some such comment as, "My cat bit my leg, so I'd better not try it." But the instructor cajoled her with praise and encouragement as well as by appealing to her fantasy family. He said, "Let's do it for George. Show him how you can do it." Such appeals were often successful in getting her to attempt the exercise. The instructor also trained her in the basic skills needed for the games her classmates played—skills like kicking and catching a soccer ball and running to a base.

The teacher tried to build Dorothy's sense of self-confidence by praising her academic and physical successes and by furnishing her with opportunities to perform orally in class and thus gain recognition from her classmates. Dorothy became the most avid and loquacious puppeteer and raconteur in the room. When given a chance, she stood before the group with a puppet on each hand and rattled on and on until halted by the teacher.

But in the area of Dorothy's fantasy life the teacher felt at a loss. The school psychologist said that there was no harm in the fantasy so long as Dorothy acted realistically in the everyday world and showed that she could distinguish the real from the dream world. Thus the teacher did nothing other than to watch the girl's reactions to classmates and to school tasks in order to estimate whether Dorothy ever seemed to confuse the actual with the imaginary.

Success of Treatment

Dorothy showed only slight progress in writing more rapidly and more legibly. Because of the brain damage that was the basis of her incoordination, progress in conquering her writing problem would necessarily be slow. The teacher worried about the way the girl's handwriting disability would interfere increasingly with her success in school as Dorothy moved to higher grade levels which demanded larger amounts of written work.

The system of assigning a classmate as a secretary to take Dorothy's dictation worked out well. Dorothy could complete her written assignments without the frustration of having to depend on a hand that only haltingly did her bidding. This classmate-system also freed the teacher to work with other pupils. In some cases a teacher who assigns an able pupil to help a disabled classmate is guilty of exploiting the able pupil, for the secretarial duties take the student away from his own learning tasks for an inordinate amount of time. But in this second grade, the teacher assigned a "buddy" to help Dorothy only for short periods once or twice a week, and on each occasion the helper was a different child.

The techniques of building Dorothy's skill and confidence in physical activities met with considerable success. At the beginning of the year she had not attempted to run. When active games were played, she had stood at a distance talking to her fantasy friends. But by the end of the school year she would enter into the kickball game, taking her turn kicking and running to base. Her gait was still slow and labored, and thus she was often tagged out. But the reward of being able to play with the others seemed to be sufficient to enable her to accept being put out without displaying anger or leaving the game.

By the close of the year Dorothy continued to spend much of her time in the dream world. However, the teacher never was able to find any evidence that Dorothy confused her fantasy life with the real world. The teacher could not decide whether Dorothy's active imagination contributed more to, or detracted more from, her overall personal-social adjustment.

CASE V: THE PROBLEM

Billy Jensen was a seven-year-old first grader in the same school that Dorothy McClure attended. By midyear it was quite clear that he was experiencing serious trouble with his academic work, particularly reading. Socially he acted more immature than his classmates. On the playground he was one of the clumsiest.

During this school year the principal and several teachers were studying the way perceptual factors related to learning difficulties. On the basis of their investigations, they decided that children in their school who were displaying motor-coordination problems could profit both physically and academically from special training to improve perceptual-motor skills.

The part-time physical-education instructor, drawing upon his training in physiotherapy, agreed in the middle of the year to set up a screening program to identify the children who most needed special work in neuromuscular coordination. The screening program consisted of five test activities administered by each teacher to her class. The activities were:

1. Stork stand (child stands on one foot with other foot at least 12 inches off the ground) to test general balance.

2. Skipping (distance of 30 feet) to indicate gross coordination.

3. Hopping (distance of 30 feet on one foot, then back again on the other) to show leg coordination and strength.

4. Ball throwing (softball tossed from one student to another 15 feet apart) to test the giving and receiving impetus.

5. Push-ups to indicate something about general body strength.

As the children performed the tasks, the classroom teacher rated each one according to simple scoring standards provided by the physical-education instructor.

Billy did poorly on the tests and was thus assigned to the special group that would receive perceptual-motor-coordination training. Before the program began, each child was given a brief physical inspection by the instructor to determine whether any of them had gross defects in posture, bone formation, and joint formation. When Billy removed his shirt for the inspection it was immediately apparent that one shoulder was held higher than the other; when viewed from the back, one shoulder blade did not match up with the location of the other.

In sum, the two problems which brought Billy to the attention of school personnel were his poor academic performance and his poor physical coordination.

An Estimate of Underlying Cause

Billy's classroom teacher was not so concerned about his future as was a young man who served as *resource teacher** for the school. The classroom teacher commented about Billy, "From my experience, boys like this grow out of their troubles. Things seem to work out eventually." But the resource teacher believed that children do not necessarily "grow out" of problems unless specific measures are taken to alter the conditions which have caused the difficulties. So he decided that if Billy were to receive special help, he—the resource teacher—would have to provide it, since the first-grade teacher was doing nothing extra to aid the boy.

* In this school district a resource teacher was an extra teacher not assigned a specific class. His duties were to aid the other teachers by securing special materials they needed, by providing remedial teaching for pupils with special learning problems, and by taking over other teachers' classes when they could profit by an hour or two away from their classrooms.

To learn more about the background of the boy's difficulties, the resource teacher invited Billy to his office on several occasions to talk, to draw and paint, and to make up stories. The resource teacher also read the information that had been compiled at the time Billy had entered school in the fall. On two occasions, this teacher talked with Billy's mother. From the foregoing sources, the teacher drew the following information:

The Jensens had moved into the district just the past summer. They had purchased a home only a block from the home of the resource teacher. By Christmas, Mr. Jensen had left the family, and the mother was in the process of securing a divorce. When Billy talked with the resource teacher during the early spring, the boy expressed dismay and unhappiness at the breaking up of the family. He said he did not know why he could not be with his father. These comments, along with the nature of the stories Billy created, suggested to the teacher that the family conflicts in recent months and the current separation of the parents were causing Billy significant emotional distress.

An analysis of the boy's difficulties with learning to read and understand arithmetic, coupled with clear evidence of his social immaturity, suggested that he was a slower developer than other children his age. His lack of physical agility could also be a symptom of late maturation. Or the physical incoordination might be caused, at least to some degree, by some internal perceptual-motor disorder of the central nervous system, and it possibly was exaggerated by the emotional conflicts the boy was presently suffering. The resource teacher could not be sure which of these possible causes was behind the incoordination. But he estimated that a program to aid Billy should emphasize attention to direct perceptual-motor training as well as to alleviating the boy's emotional distress.

Methods of Treatment

Billy was assigned to the perceptual-motor training class for two reasons: to furnish special exercises for improving his coordination and to place him in a close, friendly relationship with a man who might serve partially as a father substitute during this trying period of the boy's life. Since in his home Billy no longer had a male with whom he might identify in order to learn masculine ways of behaving, the school would try to provide some appropriate models.

The resource teacher also invited Billy to his home to play with the teacher's own two boys on Saturdays. The teacher's sons were ages four and five and thus were better matches for Billy in social maturity than were Billy's first-grade classmates. These visits also provided Billy with another male, the teacher, to serve as a model of masculinity.

Billy was assigned occasional sessions with the resource teacher at school to receive some remedial work in reading and arithmetic and to have an opportunity to express his concerns to an understanding adult. During these sessions the teacher tried to help Billy establish a clearer perception of his new life—to help the boy accept the reality of his parents' separation and the fact that many boys were in the same position. The teacher also tried to build the child's confidence in himself by giving him tasks at which he could succeed and then praising him for his success.

Success of Treatment

By the end of the year Billy had progressed in physical agility, apparently as a result of the training in coordination. But he was still one of the least nimble first graders.

He appeared to look forward with pleasure to the occasional individual sessions with the resource teacher, and he had profited somewhat from the remedial measures. But he still was far behind his more average classmates in academic work and in social maturity. Thus the resource teacher and physical-education instructor concluded that their efforts had been of some aid but that Billy's problems of incoordination, immaturity, and emotional distress were still serious ones. A more satisfactory family life, more intensive perceptual-motor training over a longer period, and perhaps more time to mature would be needed before significant improvement could be expected.

CHAPTER 10

FIVE CASES IN INTERMEDIATE GRADES

The following illustrations from grades four through six show the classroom treatment of five children whose initial symptoms ranged from temper tantrums and bullying to withdrawal from class participation and from social contact.

CASE I: BULLYING AND TEMPER TANTRUMS

The treatment of a disturbed child often consists of guessing what distorted view he holds of himself and of the world and then acting toward the child in a manner which will gradually correct his distorted perceptions. The teacher usually cannot predict accurately what event or series of events in the child's life will be most effective in readjusting his views. The case of Alex, age eleven, illustrates the fact that a long-term, consistent attitude on the teacher's part may finally be brought to observable fruition by a single event which represents a turning point in the child's development.[1]

The Problem Situation

Alex had a history of throwing temper tantrums if he did not get his way. When he entered this new classroom he was sullen and obstreperous. He was far behind his age-mates in reading, arithmetic, spelling, and similar academic subjects.

An Estimate of Underlying Cause

From the boy's belligerent attitude and his lack of attempts to succeed with schoolwork, the teacher hypothesized that Alex felt

[1] Pearl H. Berkowitz and Esther P. Rothman. *The Disturbed Child.* New York: New York University Press, 1960, pp. 120–121.

himself to be different from the other children—different in an unacceptable way. She estimated that he had hit upon bullying and causing a scene as the only way he could get much attention; even though the attention was often in the form of criticism it still made him feel important. What he needed, the teacher believed, was to recognize that he was worthy of love and acceptance and that aggressive behavior was not so rewarding as conforming behavior.

Method of Treatment

The teacher could not approve of Alex's cruel acts and had to move to stop them when they endangered others. Thus she faced a problem of gaining his confidence. She attempted to solve this problem by encouraging appropriate behavior through praising him lavishly, and sincerely, whenever possible so that he would feel valued and secure in the classroom. The teacher consistently practiced her acceptance of Alex for himself rather than rejecting him because he sometimes was aggressive. For a marked period of time there was no convincing evidence that the treatment was working.

The turning point in Alex's behavior was reached after he had indulged in a particularly stormy temper tantrum and had flung jars of paints over the room. He was not punished, however, but merely asked to mop the floor and repair the damage. His final challenge had not succeeded in making the teacher reprimand him. He was faced, for the first time in his school history, perhaps, with a situation he could not continue to handle in an aggressive fashion, for it no longer gained him prestige to be the class bully. As Alex felt that he was always accepted by the teacher, and as in acceptance lay security, he could no longer endanger that security by acting in a hostile manner. In addition, the teacher, by providing him with an atmosphere of warmth and understanding, let him know that the same feeling was expected from him in return. Alex could not tolerate the guilt feelings within him each time he felt the teacher had been the target of his aggression. To alleviate his guilt, he felt the need to conform. In conformity lay acceptance.[2]

Success of Treatment

For the first time in this grade Alex turned seriously to schoolwork, struggling with a first-grade reader and with arithmetic and spelling. Gradually his bullying techniques decreased as he obtained greater emotional satisfaction from praise and approval for his successes than his former aggression had provided.

CASES II AND III: WITHDRAWAL

These two cases are considered together in order to illustrate the fact that the same symptoms may result from somewhat different causes. If the teacher is to select an appropriate technique for treating each such case, he will find himself more successful if he bases his treatment on an analysis of the underlying cause rather than trying to apply one general treatment to every child who exhibits the same cluster of symptoms.

The Problem Situation

In a sixth-grade class two girls, Linda and Francine, brought themselves to the teacher's notice early in the year by being inattentive during class discussions, failing to complete homework assignments, withdrawing from playground activities, and remaining isolated from classmates during free time.

While deciding whether anything should be done about the girls' antisocial attitudes and what should be done about their neglect of schoolwork, the teacher observed each one more closely, talked to her individually, and phoned her mother for a conference.

An Estimate of Underlying Causes

The teacher observed that Linda seemed to be physically more mature than her classmates. She was apparently an early developer, entering adolescence before the others. Her manner of

[2] *Ibid.*, p. 120. Reprinted by permission.

dress, her hair style, and her use of facial makeup caused her to look more like an advanced junior-high girl than a typical sixth grader. During Linda's periods of psychological withdrawal from class discussions, she spent her time reading stories in magazines like *Ladies' Home Journal* and *Seventeen*. When the teacher talked privately with her about failing to do homework, Linda said that sometimes she did not understand the assignments and other times her duties at home kept her too busy to complete them. When Linda's mother came to school for the midsemester individual parent-teacher conference, the teacher asked whether perhaps together they might work out a plan which would permit the girl to complete both her duties at home and her homework for school. Linda's mother was surprised at this request. She said her daughter was only required to keep her own room neat at home, a task requiring about fifteen minutes a day. It was not home duties, her mother added, but boys, television, romance magazines, and phonograph recordings that engaged the girl's out-of-school hours. The mother explained:

> She spends quite a bit of time with these two eighth-grade girls who live near us. I don't mind her going to their houses and to the roller-skating rink, but I'm not crazy about her having a steady boyfriend at her age. He's a ninth-grade boy and seems to be nice enough, but I think she's a little young. She reads these romance magazines and ones about the new records and dance steps. I guess kids grow up faster these days.

The teacher concluded that Linda, instead of being a social isolate, was simply not interested in sixth graders, for they seemed immature to her. Far from being deprived of friendships, she was engaged in such an active life outside of school that it interfered with her responsibility for assignments. The topics of class discussions apparently bored her, and she seemed to feel sufficiently independent of adult opinion to risk the teacher's disapproving of her reading magazines during discussion sessions.

Francine, on the other hand, apparently had quite different motives for her withdrawal. The teacher observed that instead of reading during class discussions, she daydreamed, looked idly about the room, and did not know the topic under discussion when she was called on for an opinion. During free time after lunch she often read library books, usually ones about animals or Girl Scouts. Sometimes she stood at the edge of the playground watching the other pupils play, but she never tried to enter their games. When the teacher held a private interview with Francine about her schoolwork, the girl looked at her hands and simply shook her head at questions about why she did not complete home assignments.

The teacher checked the cumulative record of Francine's past school experiences and learned that she had newly entered the school in the middle of the fifth grade. She had moved to the city from a small town in Western Canada. According to notes in the record, written by the fifth-grade teacher, Francine not only had been shy, but near the end of the semester she had occasionally felt sick and had had to go home. By the end of the term she had earned low C marks in social studies, arithmetic, composition, and music. She had earned B's in reading and art.

When Francine's mother came for the midsemester conference, the teacher summarized mentally the mother's appearance: middle-aged, pretty, a bit old-fashioned in her style and dress, smiling, uneasy, apologetic. In answer to the teacher's question about Francine's missing homework, the mother said:

> She doesn't often have homework. And when she does, she usually is too worn out to do it. She's never been very well, even when she was small. And it's been hard for her moving here into a different school. She was in a very small school in Canada and rather liked it. But your school is so large. She hasn't been well lately. She's nauseated some mornings so she can't eat breakfast. Last week she broke out in hives while waiting for the school bus, so she had to come home again, and in about an hour the hives were all gone.

Asked about the girl's friendships, the mother said Francine spent most of her time at home looking at television, painting in coloring books, or occasionally playing with some second- and third-grade girls who lived nearby.

From the foregoing information the teacher estimated that Francine's withdrawal from her classmates, her neglect or rejection of class discussions and home assignments, and her illness were perhaps all results of her feeling inadequate to cope with her new life in a large elementary school and in a crowded urban neighborhood. The teacher also tentatively guessed that the girl had unconsciously learned to use illness as a method of escape from facing difficulties, and the mother's highly sympathetic attitude and overprotection only encouraged the girl to continue using illness as an adjustment mechanism. The nausea and hives were not necessarily caused by fear of school, but they might well be. The failure to take assignments home, or to complete those which she did take, also supported the theory that school was a threat which the girl hoped to avoid.

In sum, the first girl, Linda, appeared to have a too-lax conscience, as far as school responsibilities were concerned, and her heterosexual needs strongly motivated her to neglect tasks which might well be important to her future progress in school. Francine, on the other hand, appeared to have strong but unsatisfied needs for feeling adequate to cope with the academic tasks and social demands faced at school; but before she could succeed with these in any permanent way, she needed to learn more adequate ways of adjusting than simply withdrawing from her problems.

Methods of Treatment

Because Linda had secure social relationships outside of school, and apparently yearned for none within the classroom, the teacher made no attempts to urge her toward more sociability with sixth graders. However, the teacher did believe that the girl was potentially capable of performing well academically. Specifically, the teacher concluded that Linda would profit from broadening her reading interests, improving her writing, and developing a better understanding of social studies, particularly of current events. To accomplish these improvements, the instructor took three measures:

1. She tried to adapt reading, writing, and social-studies assignments more to the girl's immediate interests. She secured a
list of novels at the public library about boy-girl relationship
(high-school age) and about older girls entering careers as nurses,
airline hostesses, secretaries, athletes, and motion-picture per-
formers. Linda was asked to contribute oral reports to the class
about two of these books. For a creative-writing assignment, the
teacher suggested that Linda write a story with a roller-skating
rink as the main setting. When the class studied ways that people
live in various countries, Linda was asked to write a paper about
hair and dress styles in different cultures.

2. The teacher gave Linda more responsibility in classroom
discussions by having her serve as a panel chairman on two occasions.

3. She urged Linda's mother to see that homework assignments, given three times a week, were completed before the girl
was permitted to go roller-skating or to visit her friends.

The case of Francine appeared more serious and more complex,
so the teacher suggested that her mother take the girl to the
school district's psychological and medical staff for a proper
diagnosis of her troubles. At the same time, the teacher herself
tried to aid the girl, basing her treatment on her own estimate of
Francine's problem. The teacher reasoned that if Francine received from faculty and classmates alike more evidence that she
was a successful and worthwhile girl, her withdrawal mechanism
would gradually be replaced by more adequate adjustment techniques. To accomplish the desired change, the teacher took such
measures as the following:

1. When the class was ready to study Canada, she talked to
Francine individually one noon hour, asking the girl to help introduce the study that afternoon by telling her classmates about
life in a small town in the province of Alberta. Assuming that
Francine would not want to give a formal report in front of the
class, the teacher suggested:

> If you don't mind, I can interview you about such things as
> the schools, the kinds of work men do, the houses, and what

the boys and girls do for recreation. You can tell whatever you like about these things. If we decide now about the topics we should discuss, you can be thinking of what you might like to say. I appreciate your help with this. I've never been to Canada myself.

In this way the teacher warned the girl ahead of time about the interview and allowed Francine to limit the questions to things she was able to discuss. Earlier the teacher had planned to tell Francine about the interview a day ahead, so that she could prepare at home. But on second thought, the teacher realized that Francine might worry herself sick overnight. So she warned the girl only at noon, thus giving her some time to prepare but not enough time to work herself into a state of extended anxiety.

2. The teacher made a point of commenting more frequently on whatever aspects of Francine's classwork merited approval, such as "I'd like to put this drawing on the bulletin board where everyone can see it" or "Notice how much better you are now multiplying fractions than you were two weeks ago. That's good progress."

3. In order to encourage more social contacts, the teacher asked a mature and understanding classmate, Martha, to invite Francine occasionally to join the other girls in four square, which is a game limited to bouncing a ball and does not involve strenuous running. Furthermore, when the class divided into small groups to try science experiments, the teacher placed Francine with only two other classmates rather than on a larger committee; the purpose was to encourage the girl to contribute to the group without being overwhelmed by too many extroverted classmates.

4. The teacher talked individually with Francine about the girl's reading interests. The purpose was to show that a teacher is not only a taskmaster but also can be an understanding friend.

Success of Treatment

The teacher's treatment of Linda met with mixed success. The girl appeared to appreciate the suggestions of library books to read, she took her responsibility seriously as chairman of the two panels, and she did a moderately good job of reporting on the hair and dress styles of girls in different lands. Her homework assignments were completed with regularity for three or four months, but by late spring she was again irregular in completing them, though not so seriously delinquent as in the fall. Unless she was personally responsible for a prepared role in class discussions, she continued to read a book or magazine that was placed in her lap so the teacher could not easily see it.

The attempts to help Francine academically and to aid her in feeling better accepted by the teacher were more successful than those aimed at integrating her securely into the society of her peers. The girl reacted with initial hesitation to the opportunity to be interviewed in class about Canada, but as the interview actually began she warmed to the situation and answered the questions well. The medical and psychological examinations which the teacher had recommended tended to support the teacher's estimate of Francine's problem. The girl was not in robust health, but no organic disorder was found. A weekly one-hour session for her at the child-guidance clinic was scheduled. When the teacher talked with the psychologist who worked with Francine, the therapist agreed with the approach that the teacher had initiated to aid the girl in securing a higher opinion of her own worth. Francine gradually appeared to be less withdrawn from the teacher. Occasionally after lunch or during recess she would voluntarily stop to talk, and when the teacher smiled at her in class she began smiling back without embarrassment. Her mother reported that the occasions of nausea before school had diminished but had not entirely disappeared. Francine still was absent occasionally.

On the playground Francine somewhat reluctantly accepted the invitation of Martha to play four square, but since Francine continued to maintain her withdrawn reserve even during the game, the other girls soon forgot about her and went their own way. She was not actively rejected by them, just overlooked. Since she made no attempts of her own to be friendly, she was still generally isolated from the others by the end of the year. The teacher's attempts to pair her off in committee work with different girls so as to encourage at least one secure friendship were of no avail.

In conclusion, the teacher, by studying each of the two withdrawn girls individually, discovered that the basis for their behavior was different in each case, so the method of treatment needed to be different. In each instance the teacher's efforts brought partial success, so she judged that the attempts were worthwhile. She was disappointed that she had not succeeded in establishing more secure peer relationships for Francine. She wished that there had been another girl in the class who had had interests similar to Francine's and who was likewise rather shy so that the two of them might have paired up as appropriate friends who could satisfy each other's need for companionship.

CASE IV: ACADEMIC FAILURE AND INFANTILISM

The case of eleven-year-old Mark Hurley shows how an apparent neuro-physical disorder may impair a pupil's chances for succeeding academically. The academic failure may then cause the child personal-social difficulties which themselves, in a boomerang action, further aggravate the academic difficulties. And thus the cycle continues, so the child becomes more and more confused. The case further illustrates the way that a teacher who is not fully confident that his diagnosis of the boy's problems has been completely accurate may adopt a variety of treatment techniques rather than only one, hoping that at least a few of the techniques will improve the pupil's condition.

The Problem Situation

It was in fourth grade that Mark's parents first became alarmed because the boy was so far behind his classmates in schoolwork and because he continued to retain infantile behavior that his ten-year-old age-mates had long since abandoned. At this time Mark was reading only as well as an average second-grade child. His reading retardation impeded his progress in the arithmetic, social-studies, and science activities that depended upon reading for success. But more apparent to his classmates than his academic shortcomings were Mark's loud talk, his inability to stay in his seat, his lateral lisp, his rather frequent regression into baby talk, and his pawing and pulling at those pupils around him. These infantile acts gained him a negative sort of attention. The other children laughed at him or turned away in disgust, rejected his attempts at friendship, and sometimes mocked his lisp and baby talk.

The boy's parents asked to have a school psychologist examine Mark. The psychologist determined that he was apparently of normal general ability (IQ between 95 and 100). The psychologist recommended that Mark enter the school system's summer reading clinic and that he begin attending weekly group-therapy sessions at the county mental-health clinic.

An Estimate of Underlying Cause

In the summer reading clinic Mark met the teacher who was to work intensively with him during June and July and who subsequently would serve as the instructor of the educationally handicapped class in which the boy would enroll in September. Thus the same teacher worked with Mark from one June until the next.

In the reading clinic, the instructor worked with only four pupils. Thus he was able to study Mark closely and to accord him much individual attention. To diagnose the boy's difficulties, the teacher not only used a variety of tests of general intelligence and reading ability, but he also administered a series of motor-coordination tasks and vision tests that might reveal neurophysical characteristics. On the basis of the test results and close observations of the boy, the teacher arrived at the following tentative diagnosis:

> I felt that Mark's original difficulties with learning to read had stemmed from a neuro-physical problem. He appeared to suffer from mixed neural dominance—his left eye and left ear were the dominant ones, but he was right-handed and right-footed. To manage such a dominance problem and to learn to read adequately, he needed special techniques which had not been available in his first four years in school.
>
> I assumed that as he had fallen farther behind academically during the past four years, he had lost confidence in himself. Like any child, he needed adult and peer approval and atten-

tion. But since he wasn't getting it through the usual school channels of academic success, he apparently turned back to infantile behavior—loud speech, baby talk, and pawing others. I assumed that this was his unconscious, clumsy effort to be noticed by others, even if it had to be in a negative way.

Because of Mark's failures at school, both academically and socially, he became an unsatisfactory son in his parents' eyes. The psychologist learned from talking with them that the father was obviously ashamed of the boy's poor school performance and was embarrassed by his infantile behavior. In contrast, Mark's younger sister was just the kind of girl that parents can be proud of. Mark apparently saw this and resented her, so he took out his resentment by tormenting the girl. As a result, he incurred further criticism from his mother and father.

The whole complex of events snared Mark into a cycle of failures from which he could not escape. School failure produced in the boy's mind a distorted picture of himself and of the best ways to react to his environment. In his confusion he stumbled on infantilism as a method of adjusting. This, in turn, caused him greater failure in school, and he reacted by becoming more infantile. He needed special help to break out of this circle.

Methods of Treatment

The teacher decided that Mark needed to replace his current low estimate of his own worth with a new self-concept. He needed to view himself as an able, likeable boy. The teacher thought that such a new perception would most likely result if: (1) Mark could vent his frustrations in ways that did not alienate others, (2) he was treated like a youth whose infantile tendencies would not be catered to, (3) he received neuro-physical training so he could overcome the difficulties that were apparently produced by his mixed dominance, and (4) he was given a highly concentrated remedial-reading program so that he could attack all of his academic work with more success.

To pursue these goals, the instructor adopted the following

techniques in the class for eleven educationally handicapped boys which Mark attended from September to the following June.

> I always started him on tasks at which I knew he could succeed. For example, in spelling I gave him a third-grade book. We worked on spelling in a variety of ways—hearing words dictated on tape recordings, analyzing them to understand their component parts, and writing the words in trays of sand to receive a kinesthetic experience. Mark soon was getting a perfect spelling paper each week. This made him feel like a winner, rather than the loser of former years, so he asked for a more advanced book. I put him in a fourth-grade speller, and he was able to succeed in it as well. Spelling now began to interest him.

Not only did the instructor suit Mark's tasks in all of the subject-matter areas to the boy's current level of achievement, he also made sure that the school day contained many varied activities, none of which lasted long enough to bore or frustrate the eleven pupils. The morning's activities were organized into a regular routine, so the boys would have the security of knowing what to expect. However, to prevent them from feeling pressured by *housekeeping* details that cause behavior problems in most regular classrooms (like not dropping paper on the floor, keeping desks in straight rows, not talking to neighbors, not leaving one's desk without permission), the teacher allowed considerable freedom of movement and lack of restrictions on consulting classmates. But by the very nature of the morning's sequence of experiences, problems of boys bothering others while they were working seldom arose. That is, the teacher had organized fifteen different individual activities which he called "The County Fair." This title indicated that each activity or task was like a "booth" in a given section of the room. Following the morning's spelling program, the boys would start their rounds of the booths, with every boy assigned to a different activity. The experiences were designed to develop different skills that all of the boys appeared to need in improving their reading, perception, motor coordination, language usage, listening skills, and abilities to express themselves in art media. After a boy worked for fifteen minutes at one activity, he moved to another. In this manner the morning proceeded until each boy had been able to work at each activity. The teacher served as supervisor, moving from one pupil to another, giving special and more extensive personal help where needed.

The round of activities consisted of the following: a table containing the Dolch word games to develop reading skills; another for the Leavell stereo-reader; a third for the Frostig work sheets to aid in neuro-physical coordination; a fourth with Science Research Associates reading-laboratory materials which the pupils perused with special eyeglasses that forced them to practice reading with one eye at a time so as to develop the functional use of both eyes; and a fifth with a typewriter that afforded practice in visual-motor coordination while the pupil created a poem or story. A sixth activity was a "whisper tape," that is, tape-recorded passages of reading material spoken in whispers to help pupils increase their ability to discriminate sounds. Interspersed among the tasks which required close concentration were ones permitting them free physical expression in the forms of finger painting and easel painting. A further activity in the morning's rounds was the viewing of film strips. The rest of the booths contained similar tasks which improved reading or language skills or permitted free expression of feelings in a socially acceptable manner.

The teacher described the purpose behind the County-Fair routines in this manner:

In the past, all of these boys have had unsatisfactory school records. Almost all have been reading problems for their teachers. And since they were not able to read successfully, during reading period in their regular classes they often would turn to mischief. As a disciplinary measure that would ensure that they didn't bother their classmates, their teachers almost invariably sat them off in a corner. All of them have a long record of sitting in corners, supposedly concentrating on a challenging academic task, but actually they were bored and confused. But in our class, they have a good deal of variety. Even if they don't enjoy very much the task they're working on at the moment, they know that in just fifteen minutes they will be at another one they enjoy more. This makes the morning pass quickly. We don't have behavior problems, because they are all actively learning all the time.

Because these educationally handicapped boys had tended in the past to meet more frustrations than most other children, they also had become accustomed to bursting forth in aggressiveness of one kind or another. To permit them to vent such feelings in a socially acceptable manner, the teacher had provided two devices. The first was a punching bag which hung at one end of the room. It was not the air-filled type the size of a volleyball, but rather the large, cylindrical, sand-filled canvas "heavy bag" which professional boxers use. When Mark felt like poking or pawing a classmate, as had been his habit, the teacher reminded him to punch out his feelings on the bag instead. The second device was plastic clay. Each boy kept a chunk in his desk. When he felt like grabbing or twisting something, he took out the clay and kneaded it rather than poke a neighbor. Early in the school year Mark had turned often to these two outlets for tension. By May he seldom found them necessary, nor did he alienate classmates anymore by pawing them.

The teacher provided the neuro-physical training which Mark and many of his classmates needed by furnishing a variety of coordination exercises, such as walking on balance beams, running an obstacle course as if they were training to be commandos, and carrying out eye-hand coordination activities.

Although the boys' morning experiences were mostly individualized ones, the afternoon activities were carried on by the group as a whole. The boys played games both indoors and on the playground, and they conducted work projects related to their social-studies program. For example, during a unit on Colonial America, they built wooden muskets and dramatized scenes from Colonial history for other fifth- and sixth-grade classes. The physical activities—games, work projects, dramatics —which formed a portion of the afternoon's program were included primarily for their therapeutic effect on the educational retardates.

Mark's infantile behavior came in for some special attention.

The teacher believed the infantilism would be relinquished if the boy gained a better self-concept through classroom success and if his baby ways were not catered to—that is, if he were treated consistently like an older person. In keeping with this hypothesis, the teacher systematically encouraged self-reliance.

> If he fell down on the playground and began whining about it, I didn't fuss over him but let him accept the bumps the way an older boy is expected to. And I didn't leap to his aid in his frequent bids for attention during the class sessions. Early in the year he often came to me with some such problem as, "My pencil's broken." I would answer, "Well, then, you've got a problem." If Mark didn't respond to this, I would ask, "What do you plan to do about it?" He would finally answer, "Guess I'll have to sharpen it."

In his studies Mark would readily seek the teacher's aid when the answer to a problem did not immediately come to mind. The instructor encouraged him to look at the problem again, and when Mark came up with the solution, the instructor pointed out, "You did that yourself. I didn't do it. You did, and you did it well."

Not only did the teacher suit tasks to Mark's current achievement level and compliment the boy on his successes, but he gradually tried to help Mark face his shortcomings honestly and attempt to improve. They agreed that the teacher should signal Mark when the boy was getting too loud or was pawing a classmate or using baby talk. In this way Mark consciously took part in planning the changes that were to be brought about in his behavior.

Parallel with the foregoing classroom experiences, Mark attended weekly sessions at the county mental-health clinic. There he took part in personal interviews with a therapist and worked together with other children in art and construction activities.

Success of Treatment

Mark's year—including the summer reading clinic and the educationally handicapped class—was one of significant success, both in academic progress and personal-social adjustment. He had entered the summer clinic with the reading skills of an average second grader. By the end of the year he was reading as well as a beginning fifth grader. He had worked his way up into the fifth-grade spelling book. In the middle of the school year another of the boys in the special class had progressed so well in arithmetic that he was able to move to a regular classroom for that subject each day. By February, Mark felt sufficiently confident to ask the teacher whether he too might try the arithmetic of a regular fifth-grade classroom. He was given this chance. And although he had to enter the fifth grade's lower arithmetic group, he did manage to hold his own. So every day until the end of the semester he moved into the regular class during arithmetic period.

As Mark experienced increased success, his self-concept obviously improved. He began to attack his school tasks with greater assurance and increased interest. He began attempting problems which he would have avoided a few months earlier. Most of his infantile mannerisms disappeared. Once in a while, after suffering an emotional upset caused by an argument on the playground, he reverted to baby talk. But by June these occasions had become rare.

The boy's parents were delighted with the gains he had made in school and with his more mature behavior at home. Now that Mark was a more satisfactory son, his father began taking him on hikes and to ball games. Mark told his teacher about these occasions with obvious pleasure.

In contrast to all of the foregoing gains, Mark's lateral lisp showed no improvement. One speech therapist had worked with him for a short time, then concluded that there was no hope of correcting the defect. Another therapist said that when the psychological problems in Mark's life had been solved, the lisp could readily be eliminated through a simple training program. This therapist believed that the lisp, like the baby talk, was an infantile adjustment mechanism to which the maladjusted boy desperately clung in his confused attempts to deal with his world.

But while the other infantile mannerisms abated during the

year, the lisp remained as pronounced as ever. The teacher was at a loss for ways to help. But at the close of the year, he observed that:

> The lisp doesn't seem to embarrass Mark. And the other pupils don't mock his speech anymore. So perhaps the lisp doesn't have the negative effect on him that one might expect it to. He's made so much progress this year that he no longer needs to attend the mental-health clinic, and he'll be ready to enter a regular sixth-grade class next fall. He'll go to summer school again to continue intensive work on reading, and that should help him start off right in the sixth grade.

> His battle isn't over. He's still a vulnerable boy. If he faces school tasks that are much too difficult for him, and if he is not gradually pressed to be more self-reliant, he could revert to his old ways.

CASE V: SOCIAL AND EMOTIONAL FRIGIDITY

Just as the adult who invests in a business venture risks the possible loss of his money, so the child who invests love risks emotional wounds if the recipient of his love does not respond in kind. It seems obvious that if love is unrequited and the heart is broken, the injured investor will attempt to protect himself from another painful experience of this kind. That is, he develops adjustment mechanisms to handle future threats to his emotional investments. One logical device he may adopt is to build a psychological barrier around his emotions. Barbara Stevens, an eleven-year-old sixth grader, apparently had done this. Social and emotional frigidity fortified her against another agonizing emotional wound like those she apparently had suffered in the past.

The Problem Situation

Barbara drew the sixth-grade teacher's attention because the girl never spoke to him or to her classmates except to answer a direct question. And even in response to a question, she would only nod or shake her head if a yes or no answer would suffice. When a reply required more elaboration, she answered in a monotonous voice and, as far as possible, in monosyllables. She never appeared to display any emotion—elation, anger, excitement, sorrow, or contentment. Her problem was not one of scholarship. Her academic work was always done promptly and skillfully. She was what some teachers would consider a "nice, quiet girl." But this sixth-grade teacher was worried about her emotional numbness.

An Estimate of Underlying Cause

When the teacher inquired about Barbara at the school district's central guidance office, he learned that the previous year the fifth-grade teacher had brought the girl to the school psychologist's attention for the same symptoms of social aloofness that were now displayed in sixth grade. The psychologist, in talking with Barbara's mother, learned that the girl had never been a very demonstrative child. But her attitude of marked social estrangement had not blossomed into its current exaggerated form until Barbara was in second grade. At that time her father, a biologist at a college in New England, had left for ten months on an overseas research assignment. When he had returned home, Barbara would not speak to him. At about this same time she also had adopted her present reticence at school. Her mother had taken the girl to a clinical psychologist. Following the initial interview with the clinician, she had told her mother in firm, cold tones, "Don't *ever* take me to a psychologist again."

The Stevens family had moved to their present Midwestern location the summer before Barbara entered fifth grade. Her father was now on the staff of the local technological college.

At the request of the fifth-grade teacher last year, Barbara had met with the school psychologist, who later reported that "She was polite but very distant. I couldn't get through to her at all."

This year the sixth-grade teacher had met Mrs. Stevens on several occasions at school functions. He had observed that she was herself politely communicative but carefully controlled. Barbara's manner looked like an exaggerated version of her mother's general social-emotional style.

From the foregoing information, the teacher estimated that Barbara had been emotionally injured in the past through having invested her love in someone—ostensibly in her father, but more likely in both parents—who had not reciprocated the love as the child had hoped. It seemed reasonable that her father's long absence had been interpreted by the girl as a rejection of her. To protect herself from further pain, she apparently had adopted a frigid facade that permitted no further emotional transactions with an untrustworthy world. Perhaps her original model of aloofness had been her mother.

Although the teacher could construct the foregoing hypothesis from the scraps of data he had obtained, he felt that the girl's problem was really buried in a much more complex intrafamily relationship than he could picture with the evidence at hand. Perhaps the husband and wife were enduring an unhappy, strained relationship with each other. Possibly the home was often disturbed by verbal battles between the parents. But since the teacher did not know for sure, he had to act on the basis of his current estimate.

Method of Treatment

The sixth-grade teacher believed that Barbara needed to revise her unduly pessimistic perception of people so that she recognized that everyone would not exploit her love. She needed to distinguish between those who are cold and untrustworthy and the others who are emotionally warm and are faithful stewards of proffered friendship and love. He hoped that as soon as she was convinced that some people were worthy of her trust, she would lower her emotional defenses to enjoy the satisfactions of exchanges of friendship and love. The teacher further believed that if Barbara were placed in more situations requiring her to talk, she would recognize that it was not only safe to express herself but that she would gain much more respect and friendship from others than she had by remaining silent.

Acting on these suppositions, the teacher inserted more speaking activities into the year's program than he had ever included before. He scheduled panel discussions, individual and group reports, and oral presentations of current events. He developed a new speech unit which required each pupil to give a prepared declamation, a two-minute impromptu talk, and a one-minute extemporaneous talk, and to participate in a round of debates. To ensure that Barbara did not feel she was being singled out for the prying attention of a meddlesome teacher, the instructor made sure that he did not require any more speech behavior of her than of any other pupil. On the other hand, he also made sure that Barbara was not passed over when her turn came to perform.

In all of his interaction with Barbara, the teacher endeavored to be friendly, smiling, and fair.

Success of Treatment

In speech activities throughout the year Barbara performed at a high level of proficiency. During the debate tournament she and her partner were not defeated until the quarter finals. Though she never avoided a speaking assignment, not once did she volunteer an opinion or response in class.

On a rare occasion she appeared to strike up enough of a friendship with a classmate to engage in conversations, but these relationships never lasted.

Only once did Barbara speak to the teacher of her own volition. On this occasion, as she approached him, the teacher was elated at the prospect of her first overture of friendship. But she only complained flatly, "Martha is in my place."

After school closed in June, the teacher concluded that his efforts to unlock Barbara's social-emotional frigidity had failed.

As far as I could tell, she was the same girl at the end of the year as she had been at the beginning. Although her mother said Barbara liked our class, the girl herself never showed it. Once in a while when I was clowning or telling a joke, she showed a bit of a smile. But that was the only hint of feelings I ever detected.

On the last day of school we held the year-end party. Everyone was excited, except Barbara. She didn't come to school at all that day. I think she couldn't bear the emotional involvement that the final graduation party would bring.

Several times since school closed I have seen Barbara riding in the car with her mother. Her mother is always driving, and Barbara is sitting in the back seat.

CHAPTER 11

FIVE CASES IN JUNIOR HIGH SCHOOL

The cases in this chapter show that the adjustment problems of some young adolescents have had their beginnings in early childhood, whereas the problems of others have been caused primarily by factors somewhat unique to the early adolescent years.

CASE I: OVERDEPENDENCY

This example illustrates one way that a teacher's interview with a parent may furnish hints to the underlying cause of the pupil's disturbance.

The Problem Situation

Janice, a junior-high-school student, did not come to the social-studies teacher's attention until the second month of school. At that time the teacher asked each student to select a current event about which to give an oral report. Janice stopped after class to ask what topic she should take. The teacher told her to use her own judgment. The girl appeared puzzled and ill at ease, saying that she wanted to do it right. The instructor suggested several topics from which she might choose. The next day Janice selected a topic, outlined her talk as the teacher had directed, and stopped after class to ask if the outline was correct. These two incidents suggested that Janice might be a girl who did not trust her own judgment. As the teacher watched her more closely during the following weeks, it became increasingly evident that Janice lacked initiative, worried over making academic or social errors, and hesitated to express any opinions of her own. Because the teacher believed that such a pattern of behavior did not serve as a good foundation for happiness or success for Janice, she concluded that the girl had a problem that needed attention.

An Estimate of Underlying Cause

In her mind the teacher labeled Janice as a case of overdependence on others' opinions and direction. During the open-house evening which the PTA held in December, the teacher talked at length with the girl's mother, who inquired about Janice's progress at school. When the teacher said, "I'm trying to encourage her to trust her own judgment rather than depend so much on others," the girl's mother volunteered some information about the sources of the girl's diffidence. She said that Janice had not been in very good health as a young child, so it was necessary to protect her closely and not let her try all the activities that other children did. When the girl had been in fourth grade, she had experienced several asthma attacks. The physician who had treated her had reported that Janice was basically much hardier than her parents had given her credit for, and that she should be encouraged to play more with other children and to take part in vigorous activities which her parents had heretofore told her she should not attempt. He had said that the girl needed more encouragement and deserved frequent compliments, because from his observation she appeared unduly shy and unconfident.

From that time on her mother had frequently told the girl that she was the smartest, prettiest, and friendliest of girls, so all Janice had to do was to show off these attributes. From the mother's description, the teacher estimated that the earlier pattern of parental overprotection was now alternating with a new and overly extravagant praise which the girl herself could recognize was not deserved. Thus Janice was not only still convinced that she was inadequate, physically and socially, but the extravagant praise further unsettled her need for a trustworthy, consistent environment—a predictable and believable reality.

Method of Treatment

The teacher decided that Janice needed three things: (1) encouragement to make her own decisions, (2) the interest of other people in her ideas and activities, and (3) adult evaluations of her abilities which she would recognize as truthful and not unrealistically lavish. The instructor recognized that any improvement in the girl's attitude would develop slowly, if at all. Thus patience would be needed in working with her. Relearning new attitudes would take time. Over a short term there might be no perceptible change.

During the rest of the school year whenever Janice came for help with a decision about school assignments, the teacher said, "Let's hear your own ideas first. Maybe I can help you judge which one is best." Or "I thought you did a nice job on that last book report. What questions about this new book do you think the other students might want you to answer? The questions may give you a clue to what you might write about."

The teacher made a point of commenting favorably about the girl's written work by jotting comments in the margins of her papers, like "This point is nicely told" or "Your handwriting is coming along fine."

Almost every day as students entered class or left it, the teacher made friendly comments about their appearance, such as "Looks like Jim has a new sweater—very good looking" or "Were you skiing over the weekend, Candy? That's quite a winter tan you have." When it was possible to make such a sincere, casual remark to Janice, she did so, like "Is that some kind of crest or emblem on those gold buttons on your jacket, Janice? They're very intriguing" or "I see some of you people carrying around novels for your English class. What are you reading in English, Janice?"

While truthfully pointing out to Janice the shortcomings in her work that needed improving, the teacher made sure that the number of encouraging comments greatly outweighed the notations about shortcomings.

Success of Treatment

By the end of the year Janice was still an unsure, somewhat shy girl. But in social-studies class, at least, she had made some progress. She still came to the teacher for opinions, but by the end of the year she more frequently said, "What do you think about this idea?" rather than "Would you tell me what I should do?" She also began to volunteer an idea occasionally during class discussion. The instructor concluded that Janice's progress toward independence was less than she had hoped it would be, but the progress was about as much as could reasonably be expected in light of the fact that Janice was only one of the many pupils for whom the teacher had responsibility. It was obvious that the parents needed help in treating the girl in a consistent, understanding manner. But the teacher felt that there was nothing she should reasonably attempt for improving the parents' behavior. In order to change their treatment of the girl, the parents would probably require some intensive clinical sessions with a psychologist. The teacher obviously had neither the time nor training to attempt such a transformation, even if she had been able to convince the parents that they needed it. She had to be content with the little she had offered the girl in class.

CASES II AND III: INDIFFERENCE

One of the most common problems faced by teachers is that of interesting pupils in pursuing the school's goals wholeheartedly. In some cases the teacher's problem is to convince a student that the assigned classwork is worthwhile—that if the student really endeavors to master it, his life will be measurably improved. In other cases the problem is not to convince the student that schoolwork is worth his attention; the student already accepts that as a fact. But what he does not accept is the idea that *he* is capable of accomplishing the work. Because of his past record of failure in school, he now carries a low opinion of his own academic ability. Since he sees himself as a loser, he has stopped trying. Of course, in many instances the teacher faces both of these problems: convincing the pupil that the work is worth his efforts and that he can succeed with it.

The two cases of indifferent pupils which we shall consider involved both of the factors noted above: a student's low opinion of school tasks and a low opinion of self. Both cases are drawn from the ninth grade of a small-town junior high school in the Southwest.

During the year that the following events occurred, fifteen teachers from the ninth grade and the senior high school were meeting once a month with a psychologist from the nearby university to investigate the feasibility of doing more to aid the culturally disadvantaged pupils in their classes. Although no teacher could be expected to study a majority of his students in any depth (every instructor faced between 130 and 180 students a day), each of the fifteen agreed to study four troublesome pupils selected from among the lowest achievers in his classes. His purpose would be to learn more about the four as individuals and thus discover whether he could develop better ways to aid them within the limitations of time and energy imposed by his having to teach scores of other students as well.

In conducting his more intensive study of four pupils, each teacher had available standardized-achievement- and aptitude-test scores, some information about their home situation, the teacher's personal observations of the pupils in class, opinions that other instructors could offer when queried, and impressions gained from chatting with the students during or before class. One further device for gathering information was developed by the study group. It was a sentence-completion inventory intended to elicit students' opinions about their school and home environments, the town, their peers, their future, and things that troubled them. In order that the four students to be studied by each teacher would not feel they were being singled out for special inspection, school officials agreed to administer the inventory to all ninth, tenth, and eleventh graders. Each teacher then could obtain the inventories of the four pupils he had chosen, and the other inventories could be given to the school's guidance office for whatever use they might serve.

CASE II. THE PROBLEM SITUATION

Dave Lopez was from the 30 percent of the student body that was of Latin-American parentage. He was selected for study by his world-geography teacher because the boy seemed badly adjusted to school. Dave frequently missed class. When he was present, he seldom attempted the assigned work but would busy himself with talking to classmates or walking about the room without permission. When the teacher reprimanded him, he bristled and reacted with immediate verbal aggression. As one teacher remarked, "His temper has a very short fuse." He clearly was learning little or nothing about geography, and he disturbed the class.

An Estimate of Underlying Cause

Like many of his schoolmates of Latin-American background, Dave lived just outside of town in a small house within a cluster of identical ones. All of the houses were owned by a citrus-packing corporation which controlled a large proportion of the orange and lemon orchards of the district. The county welfare office labeled the houses "substandard." Dave's parents worked in the orchards.

Most communication within Dave's family was carried on in Spanish. Thus the world-geography teacher surmised that Dave's chances of succeeding in school were diminished by his problems with the English language. This impression was supported by the standardized-aptitude-test scores which showed Dave to be among the lowest 11 percent of the ninth graders in verbal abilities. In contrast, on the quantitative portion of the aptitude test he was at the 29th percentile.* This language problem was evident also on the achievement-test battery which found the boy scoring at the following percentiles:

Reading 15	Mathematics 30
Writing 9	Science 18
Listening 16	Social Science 31

The geography teacher thought it fair to conclude that a prime reason for the boy's poor academic performance, both present and past, was his language disability. He had never been able to read his assignments very fluently nor complete written work satisfactorily. By ninth grade he was hardly attempting them at all.

Dave's answers on the sentence-completion inventory were as follows: (The words in roman type are the sentence stems as

---

* *Percentile* means the point below which a given percent of the students scored. So the 29th percentile means that about 71 percent of the students scored higher than Dave and about 28 percent scored lower.

printed on the inventory. Words in italics are the boy's completion of the sentences.)

Directions: We are trying to suit the school to the needs of students. We can do this better if we understand what you and other students think about school, about yourselves, and about your future. The list of incomplete sentences on this sheet can help us with this understanding. Please read the beginning words of each sentence below, then finish the sentence with whatever words that first come to your mind. Do not use names of people in your answers.

1. When I finish high school *I would like any other work.*
2. The best thing about school is *dances and field trips.*
3. A real friend *would be my car.*
4. The boys that I like best *All boys are friends to me.*
5. The girls I like best *All girls are friends to me.*
6. If I could change my looks *I would be the same way.*
7. I feel like giving up when *the teachers get on my back.*
8. I would like to *finish school.*
9. In the future *I would like to work in places like an airport or ship port station.*
10. I can never be *the worker I wanted to be. I always wanted to go to collage and become lawyer or dotor to make my family look better. Because all my life my family have had money problems.*
11. The biggest trouble with school is *start to early.*
12. Most people don't like *boys or girls who dress different or wear dud jackets. I've put one on myself and police and other people kept their eye on us. The look at us has if we were going to kill them or rob them.*
13. This town is *"great" just like I would like any other town.*
14. The older I get, the more *I wonder about my future.*
15. I am happiest when *I have money and a girl and car.*
16. I am very good at *I'm not really good at anything (Maybe Drawing)*
17. I am not very good at *school work I'm below in everything.*
18. The thing I want most *would be my car.*

19. I am afraid that *I'll end up with nothing in my future.*
20. At school I feel *pretty good. I feel most all the time.*
21. At home I feel *pretty good. I feel happy with my parents.*
22. My parents are *vary good to me. I like them alot.*
23. Teachers are *pretty good. (I guess?)*
24. A family should *buy a new house and car.*
25. When I am absent I *take it easy (every easy)*

From the sentence-completion inventory the geography teacher gained the impression that Dave had a warm dedication to his family, that he liked school for its social rather than academic opportunities, and that he had a low opinion of his own academic abilities. As the teacher searched for some positive point to use as bait for enticing the boy into more productive classroom activity, he centered on item 16 in which Dave had hesitantly suggested that he had some skill in drawing.

Method of Treatment

The instructor saw little chance of doing anything in geography class to remedy the boy's language disabilities, so he set up three more modest goals to pursue: those of having Dave (1) learn at least a little something about geography (which he was not doing under present conditions), (2) stop disturbing the class, and (3) gain a better opinion of himself as a student so that he would be happier and feel less need for aggressive reactions to school personnel and academic activities.

As a start, the teacher planned to talk with the boy individually and attempt to build on Dave's apparent interest in art. While the students were completing a reading assignment at their desks, the instructor chatted with Dave about map making. He provided the boy an outline map of Europe and asked if he would color in certain countries and label them. Dave accepted the task and worked at it with true involvement, copying the names of the countries in a decorative lettering style and shading them with colored pencils. By the end of the next class period the map was complete. The instructor commented on the clear, artistic lettering, marked the map with an "A, Excellent," and displayed it on the bulletin board. The next day when the teacher asked Dave to do another map in class, the boy agreed and set to work. When the second one was nearly done, the teacher looked it over and pointed out that the second N in ENGLAND had been omitted. A few moments later he caught Dave snipping into the map with scissors. The boy was trying to destroy his faulty work rather than take the pains to correct the error. The teacher showed him how to eradicate the mistake with an ink eraser, then correct the misspelling. The result was respectable, though less than perfect. The second map earned another A and a place on the bulletin board. The following day the teacher provided an outline map of another area of the world, and the work continued.

Success of Treatment

Within a month after launching the boy on the career of map making the teacher could report that his three limited goals were being accomplished. Dave was learning the location of a variety of nations and was mastering the spelling of their names, though he still knew little about the nations themselves. He came to class more regularly. He seldom wandered about the classroom or disturbed the other students with chatter. To some extent he appeared less aggressive.

Compared to the average ninth grader, Dave was still an inadequate geographer. But compared to his wholly unsatisfactory classroom performance during the earlier months in ninth grade, his current performance was a remarkable improvement.

The geography teacher reported the effectiveness of the drawing approach to Dave's general-science and industrial-arts teachers, suggesting that they too might be able to use the boy's art interests as bait for interesting him more in the work of their classes.

CASE III: THE PROBLEM SITUATION

Linda Tatum was labeled a poor-adjustment case by her teachers because the girl was frequently truant, was irresponsible about homework and about caring for school materials, and was not working up to her apparent ability.

Her homemaking teacher assessed the problem in these words:

> She's a rather bright girl, even brighter than her test scores indicate. But she does poor work most of the time. She could be a rather attractive girl, though she's a little heavy. She doesn't make the most of her appearance. Her clothes are badly chosen, and she doesn't look very neat and clean. In other words, she's operating way below her potential, both academically and in physical appearance.

An Estimate of Underlying Cause

Among the fifteen teachers in the special study group, two selected Linda for attention. The two were the woman who taught homemaking and the man who taught general science. To arrive at the following estimate of the causes for the girl's problems in school, they pooled the information they had at hand.

Linda, age 15, lived with her father and her most recent stepmother. The girl did not appear able to confide in either of her parents. For want of someone to talk to about her concerns, she turned to her girl friends and to the few teachers who she was convinced would not laugh at her or divulge her confidences. "I've had so many stepmothers I can't count them," she told her homemaking teacher.

Linda's closest girl friends, Nita and Helen, were two of the school's most consistent truants. Though Linda attended class more often than her girl friends, she frequently disappeared from school after the morning session to join them in riding around with older boys (high-school dropouts) and in playing at the beach. Helen and Nita apparently were not the models of behavior which Linda's father thought best, for one day while chatting with her science teacher before class Linda said, "My dad says I can't go with Nita anymore, but he's so busy with his own things he'll never know if I do or don't."

Both the homemaking and science teachers agreed that Linda would be better off with different companions than Nita and Helen. Though Linda would not do homework, she would apply herself with some diligence to classroom assignments if her teacher was one she liked. But Nita and Helen disdained any work that required care or thought. The science instructor said, "They'll scribble a bit and then just sit, but Linda will work."

An incident before school in the science classroom illustrated both the quality of Nita's influence on Linda and the confidence that Linda had in the science teacher as a friend. The two girls were whispering and giggling about their experiences during the spring vacation of the previous week. When the teacher asked, "What's got you two so excited?" Linda came up and whispered in his ear, "Nita isn't a virgin anymore."

Linda's aptitude-test scores indicated that she had more ability than showed up in her achievement, a fact her teachers had observed on their own. In verbal and quantitative aptitude she scored at the 53rd percentile, or slightly above average, but her achievement-test scores averaged the 25th percentile (mathematics 41, reading 32, science 8, social science 14, writing 17, and listening 39).

The girl's answers on the sentence-completion inventory supported the teachers' impressions that Linda felt alienated from her parents, from the academic concerns of school, and from most school personnel. Her hopes and joys centered on her boyfriend and prospects of marriage.

1. When I finish high school *I'm getting married.*
2. The best thing about school is *break and lunch.*
3. A real friend *is one who'll stick by you no matter what and keep secrets.*
4. The boys that I like best *are boys that are fun to be with.*
5. The girls that I like best *are fun and keep secrets.*
6. If I could change my looks *I'd have a good shape.*
7. I feel like giving up when *the dean of students doesn't believe me.*
8. I would like to *quit school.*
9. In the future *I want a husband and family.*
10. I can never be *fond of school.*
11. The biggest trouble with the school is *the day is to long.*
12. Most people don't like *our group.*
13. This town is *boring.*
14. The older I get, the more *I want to be free.*

15. I am happiest when *my boy friends in town.*
16. I am very good at *baby sitting.*
17. I am not very good at *getting along with my parents.*
18. The thing I want most *is for my boy friend to come home.*
19. I am afraid that *I'm stuck in school.*
20. At school I feel *bored.*
21. At home I feel *even more bored.*
22. My parents are *stupid.*
23. Teachers are *about 3 in every school OK.*
24. A family should *be happy together.*
25. When I am absent I *usually ditch.*

Method of Treatment

The science and homemaking teachers believed that Linda needed: (1) to gain more success with schoolwork so she would feel less alienated from school, (2) to be close to one or two adults who were obviously interested in her welfare and could be trusted with her confidences, (3) to improve her appearance so she would be more acceptable to the kinds of students who might be a better influence on her than Nita and Helen were, and (4) to sever her close relationship with Nita and Helen and to establish friendships with students more acceptable to the school staff.

In setting up these goals or hopes for Linda, the teachers recognized that they were imposing rather typical middle-class American values on a girl who apparently held rather different views. They admitted that Linda had the right to select her own goals, but they still felt that the aims they had chosen for her were actually the ones she herself would want if she were mature enough to see more clearly the ultimate consequences of her present behavior. In brief, the teachers believed that if she continued treading along her present pathway, she would come to an end that she would live to regret.

The science teacher took several steps to aid the girl. By engaging her in small talk and by inquiring about her interests and activities, he demonstrated that he liked and accepted her. He made it a point to smile and say hello when passing her in the corridor. Since Linda never managed to bring books back to class if they were sent home with her, the teacher kept her books and materials in a drawer in the classroom so that she was always prepared to work at least in class, even though she would not do schoolwork at home. He showed no resentment at her failure to complete homework assignments but accepted her as a full member of the class. He complimented her on the diligence which she displayed on assignments done in class.

The homemaking teacher arranged for the PTA to buy dress material for Linda when the girl said she could not afford to buy it herself. The teacher also accompanied Linda to the store to select appropriate material. So that the girl would not abandon the dressmaking project when she ran across sewing problems that she could not readily solve, the instructor made sure that Linda knew how to take each new step in the process as she approached it. During the dressmaking project the teacher had opportunities to offer the girl suggestions about grooming. Linda adopted the suggestions and notably improved her appearance. The dress, when completed, was a marked success. It fitted well and earned the girl compliments from both classmates and teachers. She was obviously proud of this visual result of a school assignment. When the teacher suggested that she would attempt to convince the PTA to finance the material for a second dress, Linda said, "No. I'll buy it myself."

Although the two teachers believed they had made some progress in encouraging the girl to apply herself to school with greater diligence, they admitted that they were helpless in regard to weaning Linda away from the Nita-Helen crowd. There was simply nothing the teachers could do. Any move to separate Linda from her cronies would have to come either from Linda's parents or from Linda herself.

Success of Treatment

The science and homemaking teachers concluded that their success had been limited. Linda clearly liked both of them. They felt that this friendship was a positive factor toward keeping her in school. In homemaking class she had gained the visible reward of improved personal appearance. In science she had earned the rewards of higher marks and compliments from the teacher, who was a male adult whom she apparently admired.

On the negative side, Linda still *ditched* school once every week or two, at least in the afternoons. Her friendship with Helen and Nita appeared as strong as ever. The science teacher commented hopefully, "Maybe it will correct itself next year. The way Nita and Helen are going now, they'll drop out of school before long, and with them gone Linda may find some better company."

CASE IV: ESCAPE INTO BOOKS

When a sixth grader graduates from a typical elementary school to enter a typical junior high, he finds himself facing an environment quite unlike any he has known before. Some pupils, following the initial jolt of entering this new kind of school, readjust quickly and enjoy their stimulating new life. But for many others, junior high school is a confusing and sometimes frightening place. The new environment demands changes in the pupils' perceptions of school and of themselves that are difficult to make. We can identify several obvious reasons that the educational and social climate of the junior high usually differs markedly from that of elementary school.

First, the teachers tend to be more impersonal. They usually concentrate more on presenting their subject matter than they do on learning about the unique personalities and backgrounds of their pupils. When we realize that a typical junior-high instructor faces 140 to 180 different students a day compared to the 30 to 35 faced by an elementary-school teacher, we recognize that much of the impersonality is inevitable. But it is not only the greater numbers of students which cause junior-high teachers to give less attention to individuals. The type of college training they typically have received encourages them to give more attention to their subject matter—their college academic major—than to understanding human development and personal-social adjustment.

Second, more homework is assigned in junior high school, and students are required to be more self-reliant than they are in elementary school.

Third, the pupil who enters seventh grade is faced with larger numbers of students, ones of more varied social-class backgrounds, and ones who are at a more advanced developmental stage than any of those in elementary school. The new seventh grader, who in elementary school was one of the largest and most honored pupils as a sixth grader, is now often dwarfed by eighth and ninth graders who are the size of adults. As the new student passes from class to class each hour, he is swept along the corridors by hordes of larger, more boisterous youths. Furthermore, the newcomer may often taste the bitter scorn and apparent insensitivity of his adolescent schoolmates. It is not uncommon for the youths who populate junior high schools to display a brashness, worldliness, and ruthless humor that amaze and offend the callow new arrival.

It should be no surprise, therefore, that many seventh graders feel rather maladjusted during their first weeks or months in secondary school. Their customary view of life and their adjustment techniques, which suited an elementary-school environment, may be less adequate for the new setting. And unless they can recast their viewpoints and develop new techniques, they may continue as poorly adjusted youths throughout their high-school careers.

Case IV illustrates the way one emotionally vulnerable girl buckled under the pressures of entering junior high. The case further shows the way a teacher, who was both a physical-education instructor and part-time counselor, attempted to help the girl cope with problems in academic work, in physical agility, and in personal-social relations.

The Problem Situation

Alice Krothwall was a pretty, blond twelve-year-old. She was always well dressed in the latest teen-age fashions. She usually wore glasses.

During her first nine weeks in seventh grade, Alice did not draw much teacher attention. Those instructors who did notice her recognized only that she did not look directly at them or at the blackboard, responded to questions willingly but in a weak voice, and did a poor job on written work. If any of them did think Alice might need special help, they apparently believed somebody else on the staff was looking after her.

One teacher, however, was seriously concerned about the girl. It was the girls' physical-education instructor who served part time as a counselor. She had been acutely aware of Alice's social ineptness and physical incoordination since the first week of school. No matter what the physical-education activity, Alice always turned in the poorest performance. Though she always tried conscientiously, she failed miserably. In volleyball when she held the ball in her left hand and tried to serve it with her right, she missed the ball. She was the slowest runner and the poorest catcher. During the early weeks of the semester the other girls laughed at her awkwardness and taunted her. By the end of the semester she no longer amused them. They simply ignored her.

Alice had no friends. Though she was a pretty girl with a good figure, she continually hung her head as if embarrassed. This habit gave her poor posture. She never spoke unless spoken to. She never looked directly at the person with whom she was talking. Instead, she looked at the ground or cocked her head at an odd angle to glance off to the side. During noon hour other girls and boys poked her or taunted her. One girl called out, "Don't you want a date with my little brother?" This made the crowd laugh. In mathematics class a girl was overheard telling her classmates, "I'm charging just a nickel to look back there at the blond kook."

When midterm grades appeared at the end of nine weeks, Alice received five D's and two C's. It was not that her teachers thought she was lazy. Rather, they thought she tried but could not succeed. Thus she received satisfactory "classroom citizenship" marks while earning unsatisfactory academic marks.

The physical-education teacher, now performing in her role of counselor, set out at this midterm point to try to find a better solution to Alice's problems than the school was currently providing. The teacher studied the records from elementary school, talked with Alice's other teachers and with the girl's mother, and talked with Alice herself on several occasions. The English instructor said, "She needs a thorough grounding in basic fundamentals." The art teacher said, "She drifts off into daydreams much of the time and forgets what she's supposed to be doing."

Alice's problems were obviously complex. Her academic progress, personal-social relationships, and physical appearance and coordination were all unsatisfactory.

An Estimate of Underlying Cause

By reading the cumulative-record folder from elementary school, the teacher-counselor learned that Alice's social and academic problems were not new. In third grade Alice's mother had requested that a school psychologist study the girl because of her slowness in learning and her difficulties in getting along with other children. Alice's classmates had laughed at her because she had seemed unable to distinguish between reality and fantasy. Her only friends had been those created in her fantasies.

The psychological study at the third-grade level suggested that Alice's parents had shielded her too much from active social contact with other children, so Alice apparently had received too few opportunities to learn suitable techniques of social interaction.

Standardized reading and arithmetic scores, reported as percentiles, from grades four through six had been:

	Grade 4	Grade 5	Grade 6
Reading	19	61	46
Arithmetic	21	50	25

In seventh grade after Alice received the low midsemester marks, the teacher-counselor asked the girl's mother whether she would like a psychologist to meet with Alice and try to diagnose more accurately the nature of the problem. Mrs. Krothwall agreed, but she said she did not have much hope because after the diagnosis had been made in third grade the psychologist had seemed to lack any concrete suggestions about how to help the girl.

The new psychological examination showed that Alice performed much better on individually administered tests than she did on the group tests taken in school. She did best on the word-meaning items, on which she scored as high as the average tenth grader. Her scores in other areas, such as quantitative relationships, were considerably lower. This did not surprise the psychologist, for when he asked what she did in her spare time at home, Alice told him, "I go in my bedroom and read." When he asked what else she might do, she said, "I might go into the garden and hide under a bush. I might take my doll with me."

When the teacher-counselor consulted Alice's other seventh-grade instructors, she learned that the girl consistently retreated into a book when faced with problems in class. Whether she was supposed to be solving mathematics problems or participating in Spanish grammar drills, Alice frequently was observed furtively reading a book she held in her lap. But since this particular escape technique caused no trouble in class and seemed to reflect a desirable academic bent on Alice's part, she had been allowed to get away with it.

One aspect of the case that was particularly puzzling was the fact that Alice had earned A's and B's in sixth grade, yet she barely managed to get D's in junior high. The teacher-counselor phoned Alice's former sixth-grade teacher and learned that he had dedicated a great deal of attention to the girl, providing her the personal support and constant guidance that had enabled her to succeed. The grades he had awarded were also apparently inflated somewhat by his effort to make Alice feel more adequate and self-assured. The teacher-counselor, learning of the personalized attention accorded to her in sixth grade, now recognized what a blow this vulnerable girl apparently had suffered in entering the impersonal, competitive junior high.

In trying to sum up the probable causes behind Alice's difficulties, the teacher concluded that:

1. The physical incoordination might be seated in some type of brain injury that had occurred early in the girl's life. But the sheltered life that Alice had led and the emotional tension that seemed to build up when she had to contend with other children may have contributed to her physical ineptitude.

2. The seeds of her exaggerated shyness could not be identified. They apparently lay in the distant past. They probably had developed from the style of social interaction established between

Alice and her parents in her earliest years. Possibly her parents had feared so much for her welfare that they had greatly over-protected her from attempting physical and social feats that they considered daring but which in truth were ones which all normal children must attempt in order to gain experience and confidence in their own abilities. But this was only conjecture. The teacher could not know for sure.

3. Alice apparently had turned to books for solace and excitement since she had no friends of her own and did not perform interesting deeds in her real life.

4. The academic failure was probably caused by a complex of factors: low self-esteem, emotional blocking that arose from disturbed personal-social relations, and possibly some perceptual-neural disorders resulting from brain injury. The teacher-counselor gave particular attention to the emotional factors and estimated that apparently Alice's lack of self-confidence in other areas of her life affected her approach to school tasks. When faced by difficulties, her style of life had been to escape into books rather than strive hard to overcome the difficulties directly. In sixth grade a conscientious teacher had kept close watch over her progress and was able to encourage her when she faced problems. He could pace the tasks so that none was too difficult for her to tackle. But in the impersonalized junior high, she was on her own. When faced with difficulties in schoolwork, she could not press herself forward with her meager supply of self-confidence, so she turned again to the easy way out—books.

Method of Treatment

Since the teacher-counselor believed that Alice's high marks from sixth grade had misled the junior-high staff into placing the girl with students too advanced for her, Alice was moved out of the high-average section into a low-average class. The counselor hoped that Alice would thus face competition with which she could contend. In addition, the counselor talked with the girl's new instructors and described Alice's tendency to escape into books when she faced problems. The instructors were asked to treat the girl kindly, but to be firm about insisting she work at

each assignment until completed. They were also asked to give
her recognition for whatever successes she might achieve, so that
she might begin to picture herself as a success rather than a
failure.

In regard to Alice's social isolation, the counselor felt that
school personnel could do little to help. In the counselor's words:

> I can't force others to like her. If I asked the other girls to
> befriend Alice, they would simply resent my interfering with
> something they regard as their own affair. The best we can do
> is to see that she has opportunities to be with other girls under
> circumstances best suited to fostering friendship. Then she has
> to earn friendship by being friendly herself. I've suggested to
> her mother that Alice occasionally invite a girl over to spend
> the night. If Alice could develop a bond with even one girl,
> she would be so much better off.

Mrs. Krothwall took this suggestion and on several occasions
did invite a schoolmate to stay overnight.

The counselor, in her own physical-education classes, tried to
arrange Alice's activities so that the girl would gain some physical
skill but would not alienate other girls with her inaptitude. Thus
in team sports, Alice was given the task of aiding the referee and
keeping score rather than being assigned to a team, where her
lack of skill would damage the group effort and anger the other
girls because Alice had lost the contest for them. During the
basketball and soccer seasons, Alice took part in pregame drills
which aided her with physical skills, but when the game started
she was given a whistle and she ran along the court or down the
field with the referee. (She could not be asked to referee because
she was so indecisive.) When the class worked on individual
activities, like stunts on the trampoline, Alice took her regular
turn with the others.

The counselor recommended to Mrs. Krothwall that Alice be
given a thorough physical examination to discover possible bases
for her perceptual-motor incoordination and, if possible, that the
girl see a psychiatrist to receive aid with her personal-social adjustment. Mrs. Krothwall willingly accepted this suggestion.

Throughout the school year Alice's mother proved to be a pleasant, willing ally in the school's attempts to aid the girl. At one point in her discussions with the counselor, the mother asked:

Wouldn't it be wise to retain Alice in seventh grade another year? I think we should have done it in an earlier grade, because she does seem so immature. But perhaps it isn't too late now. What do you suggest?

Success of Treatment

On her report card at the end of the year, Alice received five C's and two D's. The D's were in mathematics and music, where she still was unable to attack the work with enough energy to achieve acceptable grades. But in her other five classes her improved efforts were obvious. She gained public recognition in her art class when a picture she had drawn of a skunk was displayed on the bulletin board as an example of excellence. Alice told the counselor that she was very pleased by this recognition of her work. In Spanish class she now participated in oral drills along with her classmates, though she still could not bring herself to recite alone. In English and social studies she also showed measurable gains.

The attempts to improve Alice's social relationships were unsuccessful. Although Mrs. Krothwall had invited a girl to stay overnight with Alice on several occasions (a different classmate each time), Alice did not seem to enjoy the companionship. Following each visit, she freely described the shortcomings of the visitor. For instance, when the counselor asked Alice about a schoolmate who had stayed at the Krothwalls' the previous Friday night, Alice said, "She was awful about breakfast. When she saw we didn't have bacon, she acted just like a child who had been reprimanded."

One hint of slightly improved acceptance by her classmates was observed in physical-education class near the end of the semester. During trampoline exercises, Alice always performed the one simple stunt that she could accomplish successfully. Earlier in the semester the other girls either had laughed at her or had ignored her. But during May one or two would occasionally comment, "That's good, Alice" or "Nice going."

The physical examination yielded an unexpected error in judgment on the part of the physician. He found the girl to be physically sound, but at the end of the examination he made the mistake of handing her a slip of paper and telling her, "Here are the names of four psychiatrists. Your mother can pick one of them." When Alice joined her mother outside, the girl broke into tears and asked, "Am I crazy? He said I had to go to a psychiatrist." After that incident, every time mention was made of setting an appointment with a psychiatrist, Alice became very distraught. Hence her mother decided not to take her for psychiatric help until "she settles down." By summertime this visit was still being postponed.

In regard to Mrs. Krothwall's question about whether Alice should be retained in seventh grade another year, the counselor recommended that only if the girl were transferred to a different school should she repeat the grade. In her present school, it appeared that she would profit more by passing on to eighth grade with her class. If she were retained, she would need to bear the additional burden of being stigmatized as a "flunker" in the eyes of her schoolmates.

What Alice needed in the future was additional understanding on the part of her teachers, perhaps an opportunity to attend summer camp for more chances to learn to get along with agemates, and psychiatric help.

CASE V: ACADEMIC MISPLACEMENT

As noted in Chapter 2, *good adjustment* and *poor adjustment* are not two absolute conditions. Rather, each person is only relatively well or poorly adjusted. The effective school staff, recognizing this fact, does not simply wait for a pupil to display gross symptoms of disturbance before anything is done to better his lot. Instead, alert teachers and counselors are always trying to see that the school's offerings are well suited to the pupils' needs, whether or not the students are currently showing evidence of marked maladjustment.

Case V illustrates the fact that errors may be made in assigning students to classes as they first enter a large secondary school which must process masses of students at the beginning of the school year. The case further shows one way that a teacher who is sensitive to the possibility of such errors can, on her own, identify pupils who should be moved to a more appropriate class.

The Problem Situation

On the basis of his low entrance-test score in reading skills, David Schmidt was placed in one of the seventh grade's special classes for poor readers. The number of students assigned to each of these special-reading classes was limited to fifteen so that the teacher could give them more individual attention than was possible in the regular English classes, which enrolled 25 to 35 pupils.

During the first two weeks of school the teacher administered tests of specific reading skills and had each pupil read to her aloud so she could determine more precisely the students' individual strengths and weaknesses. It was through this diagnostic testing that she discovered discrepancies between David's entrance-test scores and his abilities in individualized testing. He was strong in some skills though moderately weak in others, like such word-attack techniques as phonics and the use of prefixes and suffixes. To help correct his shortcomings, she gave him special reading exercises. David applied himself diligently to these tasks and showed immediate progress. The teacher asked that a psychologist give the boy an individual intelligence test which might confirm her suspicion that he had been misplaced. The school psychologist administered the Stanford-Binet Test, on which David earned an IQ of 120, well above average.

In brief, the teacher judged that if David continued in the special reading class and in the other low-academic-level seventh-grade sections, he would not be challenged to progress at a speed commensurate with his real ability. Though David apparently did not consider himself maladjusted, his teacher believed that his current school environment did not suit his needs.

An Estimate of Underlying Cause

The reading instructor judged that three factors had caused the boy's misplacement.

First, during the mass-testing process of entrance examinations David had apparently become confused and had not performed up to his capacity.

Second, the survey test which had formed the reading portion of the overall entrance examination had yielded only a gross score of reading comprehension and thus had not revealed the way specific subskills of reading were patterned in David's case.

Third, in elementary school the instruction that David had received in specific subskills had not been very effective. Either he had not been taught word-attack skills or else he had not been receptive at the time they were taught. In any event, he had come to junior-high school with a mixture of strengths and shortcomings in reading. The rapidity with which he began to make up the shortcomings during the early weeks of school indicated that he was an able, diligent boy.

Method of Treatment

At the end of the first month of school the reading instructor recommended that David be moved immediately from the lower-level sections into a higher series of classes that would contain classmates of similar talents. Since the teacher herself taught one of the higher English sections, she asked that David be assigned to it so she could build on the analysis of his needs which she had been able to make in the first weeks of school. The guidance counselor accepted this advice and shifted David into the more advanced sections in English, social studies, foreign language, and mathematics.

Success of Treatment

At the end of the first semester in the advanced sections David's marks were all A's and B's. The guidance counselor at the end of the year summarized the case in these terms:

This boy was given the opportunity to extend himself because a teacher took the time to express her concern for his proper grade placement and because she confirmed her suspicions with individual reading tests of her own. She has continued to take an active interest in David and has undoubtedly contributed to his overall success as a seventh grader.

CHAPTER 12

SIX CASES IN SENIOR HIGH SCHOOL

As the following cases show, a teacher's assessment of a student's problem can lead to the application of quite varied treatments in different cases, such as altering the student's school tasks, giving the student advice about changing his behavior, providing public recognition in a dramatic production, or furnishing him a course of programed instruction. The teacher's decision about which of these treatments will be the most effective depends upon such factors as: (1) the student's intellectual and physical abilities, (2) the student's social and academic history, (3) the teacher's skills in personal relations, and (4) the school facilities at hand.

CASE I: MISFIT AGGRESSION

The case of Salvador Hernandez, a Puerto Rican high-school junior who moved during the summer from New York City to live in a Connecticut suburb, illustrates two points: (1) that social-adjustment techniques which are appropriate in one environment may be maladjustive in another and (2) that a teacher who is admired and trusted by a student can sometimes offer advice which the student agrees with and adopts.

The Problem Situation

During the fourth week of school in the fall, a physical-education instructor recommended to the varsity football coach a new eleventh-grade boy who was performing "like a professional" in the gym-class touch football games. The coach made a point of observing the next class. He readily agreed that the boy, Salvador, could run, pass, and block better than any of his varsity backfield men. He urged Salvador to come out for the team.

Within two weeks Salvador had earned a place on the starting team. At the same time it became apparent to the coach that dissension had arisen between Salvador and the other boys. While the team was dressing after practice one afternoon, an argument broke out in the locker room between Salvador and another player, and Salvador pulled a knife from his pocket to challenge his opponent. A player called the coach, and the threatened fight stopped when the coach appeared. During the next two days the coach talked with several players about the incident. They complained that Salvador did not fit in well with the rest. Although he was friendly much of the time, he took offense easily and sometimes pulled the knife. Other things about him also set him apart from the others: his hair was thick and long on the back of his neck, he was the only dark-skinned student in school, he wore what the others called a "black satin hoodlum jacket," he spat on the floor in the corridors, and he swore in a manner that both impressed and disturbed many of his classmates. As one boy said, "We swear too, but not like him. He's real dirty."

An Estimate of Causes

In addition to talking with several of the other players, the coach asked Salvador's English, history, and science instructors about his conduct in their classes. Each of them said the boy caused no trouble. He completed the assigned work regularly, earning B's and C's on written papers and tests.

One afternoon following the locker-room incident, the coach asked Salvador to stop at his office after football practice. They talked briefly about the success of the day's practice and about an injured player. Then the dialogue continued in this vein.

COACH: "I'm interested in the way you're getting on, coming to a new school. You're doing fine on the team, and when I talked with your teachers they said you're in good shape in their classes. Where did you go to school last year in New York City?"

SALVADOR: "On the West Side."

COACH: "You got along all right in your studies there, too?"

SALVADOR: "Yeah."

COACH: "You like school? I mean the classwork?"

SALVADOR: "Yeah. It's okay. Lot of students didn't do their work. But my folks made me do it, and I liked it all right. It wasn't too hard if you kept up with it."

COACH: "You got along all right with the other students?"

SALVADOR: "Sure."

COACH: "Were there many white students in the school?"

SALVADOR: "Not many. Mostly colored kids. Like me, a lot of Puerto Ricans."

COACH: "Quite a few gangs around your neighborhood? Fights pretty often?"

SALVADOR: "Sure."

COACH: "Most of them carry switchblades?"

SALVADOR: "Sure. Got to."

COACH: "You notice that nobody here carries a knife. And the fact that you do may cause some problems. I want to see you get along well here and like it. And that's why I wanted to talk with you, to explain what the students are like here, in case you didn't quite understand them. In the school you went to before, you got along well with the students because you acted the way they did. You fitted in. But now when you come to this school, some of the ways you learned before don't fit. This upsets the students here. They don't know for sure how to take you. When you pulled a knife to fight with the other day, it really threw them off. I lived part of my boyhood in a tough neighborhood in a big city, so I recognize the knife as a normal weapon in the kind of neighborhood you came from. But it isn't normal here. And if you continue to carry a knife, it's going to build a wall between you and the other students. It makes them suspect you of . . . of something they don't understand."

SALVADOR: "They're prejudiced against colored people."

COACH: "Maybe some of them are, but most aren't. Teen-agers are a lot better about race prejudice than their parents. I'm sure they'd be proud to have you as a friend. It gives white kids a chance to feel they are living up to America's ideals if they have a colored friend. Race prejudice among young people isn't very popular these days. It's more acceptable not to be prejudiced."

The coach and Salvador sat silently for a minute.

SALVADOR: "So you want me to change."

COACH: "Do you think your parents will be staying in this town? Do they like it here? Are they getting along all right?"

SALVADOR: (paused in thought) "Yeah. They like it fine. They didn't like living in apartments on the West Side. Here we live in a house on property that's owned by a Mr. Fenniman. My father's the gardener and my mother's the cook for the Fennimans."

COACH: "Then you'll be in this school for the next two years. It looks to me as if you have two choices. You can make no changes to fit into the way the teen-agers act here, and you'll probably have few if any friends. Or you can change a few things, like carrying the switchblade, and become a big hero, with everybody wanting to be your friend."

They sat silently for a few moments.

COACH: "I'm not fooling you about this. If you weren't such a good athlete and if you weren't good looking and a pretty good student, I wouldn't gamble on your being much of a success here. But you have so many of these strong points in your favor, it seems a shame not to make a few changes that can help you be happier."

Salvador sat watching the floor without commenting.

COACH: "I'm not criticizing you for carrying the knife in your last school. That was obviously a normal thing to do there. It was smart. It helped you get along well. But the customs are different here. If you do some of these things the way they are used to having them done around here, you'll certainly get along well here too. (Pause.) Well, enough about that. Let's get to football. I want to show you a new screen pass we'll try out next week." He turned to diagram a football play.

As the above dialogue suggests, the coach estimated that Salvador was a talented, basically friendly youth whose peer-relationship troubles in the new school were caused by his retaining social-adjustment mechanisms which were appropriate within his former environment but, in some instances, were ill suited to the new one. The forms of aggression learned in the city school did not fit the suburban one, nor did certain patterns of speech, dress, and grooming. The coach also estimated that the boy, coming into a strange environment, would feel insecure and would be more sensitive to possible slights or rebuffs from classmates; hence Salvador would conclude the others were prejudiced against him.

Method of Treatment

The coach's attempts to do something about Salvador's peer relationships were based upon the assumption that the boy wanted to be accepted by his peers and that he would be happier if he could be welcomed into an active role in school affairs. That is, the instructor assumed that the boy's needs for acceptance and accomplishment were at present incompletely fulfilled. Thus the coach was not asking Salvador to conform to local social patterns simply for conformity's sake but rather because by changing his patterns of expressing aggression and by altering some of his personal habits, his needs would be much more adequately satisfied.

The coach first attempted to alter Salvador's perception of his current social situation, pointing out both the positive and negative aspects of it. This attempt was made by means of the conversation described above. Oftentimes such a direct, advice-giving approach does not succeed, for it is either unconvincing to the youth or else it appears to be too much of a threatening attack on an already unsteady ego. Thus direct advice risks alienating the youth from the adult. However, in other cases it does succeed in realigning the individual's view of himself in his new environment. In using the approach that he did, the coach was depending on two assumptions: (1) that the boy respected him for his prestigious position as coach and trusted him for the fairness he had displayed in providing Salvador the same opportunity as any other boy to succeed on the team and (2) that the boy was intelligent enough to recognize the differences between the expectations within his former neighborhood and the expectations within the present one. Since the instructor realized that suggestions for too many changes in behavior might place too great a task before the boy and cause him to reject any suggestions at all, the first conversation focused on only one specific item: carrying a knife. The coach hoped that by opening up the problem and by predicting major rewards of respect and friendship which adaptation to the new environment might bring, the boy would be able to see for himself that he could profit from other changes as well. The coach did, on two other occasions, suggest that Salvador not spit on the floor in the locker room or gymnasium and that he restrict his swearing to use around people whom it would not offend.

In addition to talking with Salvador, the coach spoke to several of the other players who were held in high regard by their fellow students. He explained to them that:

> As you know, Salvador is from New York City. He lived in a tough neighborhood down there and he went to a tough school. To survive there he had to develop a tough crust. He's trying hard to fit into our school, but he needs some help. He's afraid that the students here don't like him because he's colored. I know that's not true, but he doesn't know it. I think he's basically a fine boy. He just needs our friendship and help in knowing how boys are expected to act around here, and he needs some patience from us while he learns. Anything you boys could do to help him feel more welcome would be appreciated, I'm sure. You students can do more for him than any of us faculty members can.

Success of Treatment

Apparently the coach's two basic assumptions had been correct: that Salvador strongly desired social acceptance and that the direct suggestions on the coach's part would convince the boy that he could readily achieve the acceptance. After their conversation it immediately became clear that Salvador was diligently attempting to adapt himself to local patterns of adolescent behavior. The first obvious change was that he left the knife at home and did not bristle at the least remark that might be interpreted as a criticism. The second obvious change—one he initiated on his own volition—was to have his hair cut in crew style, matching the style of many of the other athletes. He began to establish an increasingly amicable relationship with peers of both sexes, but especially with his teammates, who included him in the exchange of jibes and jokes which made up much of their social intercourse. They also invited him into the gang of boys who went to the movie on Saturday night or "hung around" one of their homes or a drive-in restaurant. He was not invited to parties involving both sexes because he had no girl friend in the community. The publicity he received on the sports pages of the town's newspapers increased his stature in his age-mates' eyes and consequently increased his own feeling of worth. He apparently no longer felt it was necessary to act so aggressively.

The coach concluded that by the end of the school year Salvador's social adjustment in the suburban school was excellent, except for the continued problem that he had no girl friend. Throughout the winter and spring his social acceptability was continually enhanced, a result of his own successful attempts to act more like the suburban youth and of his notable performance on the basketball and track teams.

CASES II AND III: SOCIAL HANDICAPS

When a drama teacher casts a play, he frequently faces the decision of whether to use the play as a vehicle for aiding maladjusted students by giving them acting roles or whether to choose only students who would represent no risk to the play's complete success. This problem is not unique to dramatic coaches but is faced also by teachers who organize band, orchestra, or choir concerts, modern-dance performances, election campaigns, assembly programs, debates, and athletic events. In essence, the problem is: To what extent should the success of public performances be risked for the sake of therapy?

And if an instructor does decide to take a chance on a student whom he hopes to help by offering him a part in the play, what problems does the instructor face in convincing the maladjusted student to take the risk involved in such a public appearance?

These two issues are involved in cases II and III which show how one teacher of speech and drama attempted to combine high-quality play production with aiding two handicapped girls achieve better personal-social adjustment.

CASE II: THE PROBLEM AND AN ESTIMATE OF CAUSE

Jacqueline Stoval was a tall, graceful high-school junior who stuttered severely. She was the worst case that her speech teacher had met in his several years of teaching.

Other than stuttering, Jacqueline experienced no trouble succeeding with schoolwork. She consistently earned high marks in all classes. However, her personal-social adjustment was not the best. She sometimes seemed ill at ease in talking with classmates. Occasionally she appeared worried and kept to herself.

As in the cases of most stutterers, the underlying cause for the girl's malady was not at all clear. She was from an upper-middle-class family which expected her to succeed well in school, both academically and socially. Her parents were greatly concerned about her speech defect, and they had for some time financed individual speech-therapy sessions. In school Jacqueline was also enrolled in the regular speech class which all students took. Her teacher in that class estimated that her parents had perhaps exerted undue psychological pressure on Jacqueline to conform to high standards of performance in her preschool and primary-grade years. This pressure, applied at the time the girl was forming her basic speech habits, may have been a significant factor in causing her stuttering. But this was only speculation. The teacher had no way of learning the truth. Whatever treatment he applied to aid her would have to be based on his general knowledge of stutterers rather than on specific factors that might have caused the handicap in Jacqueline's case.

Method of Treatment

From his training as a speech teacher, the instructor recalled several generalizations about stutterers that could guide his work with Jacqueline. He knew that stuttering is a complex psychological problem. The severity of a pupil's stutter is increased by conditions that make him feel anxious. Conditions which make the individual feel at ease, accepted by others, worthwhile, and skillful tend to decrease the stutter.

People who deal with a stutterer should not pretend the handicap does not exist. Neither should they "feed" him words when he hesitates, nor should they appear impatient with him. Instead, they help him most when they frankly recognize his disorder, yet clearly accept the stutterer and patiently wait for him to express himself at his own rate.

One fact about stutterers that was of crucial importance in the case of Jacqueline was that most of them sing or recite with no hesitations at all in their speech.

As the speech teacher began to select a cast for the public performance of the comedy *The Man Who Came to Dinner,* he saw an opportunity to augment Jacqueline's self-confidence and at the same time to fill the important role of the urbane secretary in the play. The teacher later explained that his decision to offer this part to Jacqueline was not simply an act of charity that would jeopardize the success of the performance.

> She had the appearance, bearing, and intelligence that suited the part of the sophisticated Maggie of the play. I might have offered the role to several other girls who might have done it well; but I think that when you can be of special help to a capable student by giving her the chance to appear on stage, then she certainly is the one who should have the part.

When he suggested to Jacqueline that she try the role, she said, "You know, I have some trouble with my speech."

He answered, "Of course, but it will make no difference. In this play the secretary, Maggie Cutler, doesn't stutter. You'll be Maggie on that stage, and you won't stutter either. You'll be fine."

Without hesitation, the girl agreed to try.

Success of the Treatment

As the instructor had hoped, Jacqueline's performance was excellent. Her speech was flawless. Both the faculty and students were amazed. The play had provided her a unique opportunity to prove to herself and to the world that in her well-known area of weakness, speech, she had performed at a level of excellence which few of her classmates could have equaled.

The improved self-perception that resulted from her dramatic success was reflected in her everyday speech in the weeks and months that followed. It is clear that the play could not be credited for all of the improvement that appeared in Jacqueline's speech and personal relations. The individual speech-therapy sessions which she was attending also played an important part. But the speech teacher was convinced that the girl's success on the stage had been significant in bringing about her noticeably improved adjustment.

CASE III: THE PROBLEM SITUATION

The first and only Negro girl to enroll in a large high school near Washington, D. C., in the first year of the school's racial desegregation was Mary Tolliver, a somewhat overweight sophomore. Mary and two Negro boys who entered with her symbolized this suburban, middle-class community's reluctant, token recognition of the power of the Supreme Court.

Mary's problems in adjusting to the new high school began early in the year. Her speech teacher later said that among the 1,500 white students in the school there were many segregationists, including a quantity who:

> . . . behaved like idiots and treated her very badly. A few enlightened, understanding students made overtures of friendship which Mary rejected. So from the beginning, her social relations were very unsatisfactory. She isolated herself from everyone.

Her academic work was hardly any better. She was indifferent about her studies, and she became increasingly truant.

An Estimate of Underlying Cause

To find out whether something might be done through the speech class to aid Mary, her speech teacher conferred with her counselor and learned that before Mary transferred into the desegregated school she had been an above-average student with no apparent social problems. Until this year, all of her schooling had been solely with Negro children and teachers. To now be a member of a small racial minority in the school population was an entirely new experience for her.

The counselor surmised that Mary must be feeling great hostility toward—and fear of—the white students and teachers. He believed that this hidden hostility and fear were being manifested in negativism and withdrawal.

The speech teacher estimated that Mary resented being used as a tool of social justice. Probably she was indignant because her parents and the other Negroes of the community expected her to serve as a wedge to pry open the white schools and thus right a social wrong.

Method of Treatment

Near the middle of the school year the speech teacher called Mary in for a private conference. He told her he planned to produce Lillian Hellman's play *The Little Foxes.* He said that he saw a great deal of prejudice around, and he felt this drama had something important to say about the matter. He asked Mary if she would try out for the part of a Negro servant. It would require a very sensitive portrayal, because the play depended primarily on the servant's role for successfully conveying its theme. He read to Mary key passages from the play to illustrate the importance of the servant's part. He explained that the production would require long evenings of rehearsal. In the end, Mary reluctantly agreed to try out.

During the early rehearsals, the teacher-director candidly discussed with the cast the motivations of the greedy, prejudiced Hubbard family, who "ate the earth and all the people on it." He described in some detail the socioeconomic conditions that resulted from Reconstruction. As rehearsals proceeded, the cast freely discussed racial prejudice. Mary worked diligently on her own part and was also helpful to the director in interpreting the role of the rather obsequious Cal, another Negro character, who was, however, being played by a white student.

Success of the Treatment

In the final production of *The Little Foxes* Mary gave a moving performance. But more important, the opportunity to take part in the play transformed her perception of school and of many of the students and teachers. During the period of preparation for the play her attendance at school had become almost perfect. Her grades improved in spite of the rehearsal hours. She made friends among other members of the cast and stage crew, and during the following two years in high school she remained active in the drama club. In her senior year she was elected drama-club president.

Following graduation from high school, Mary enrolled in the state university and prepared to teach speech and drama in a secondary school.

CASE IV: A CONFLICT IN OBJECTIVES

In some instances the apparent maladjustment of a high-school student is more accurately labeled a maladjustment of the school curriculum. The typical college-preparatory course is not well suited to the student's needs, abilities, or vocational desires. In these cases it is not so much that the student needs changing as it is that the school program needs improving.

The Problem Situation

Eddie was a large, friendly, good-looking sixteen-year-old high-school sophomore who frequently missed school because he served as a substitute driver for his father's trucking firm. In the American literature class which he was taking to fulfill the sophomore English requirement, Eddie never did any of the homework. In class he usually paid a moderate amount of attention to the discussions, but he never could add anything to them except an occasional humorous remark. If asked whether he had read the assignment, he would laugh with scorn and say, "That stuff?" or "Not this boy—I'm too busy."

An Estimate of Cause

The English instructor was sufficiently irritated by Eddie's lack of effort and his smart-alec comments to look up the boy's past performance which was recorded in the school's cumulative-record file. The academic record showed that Eddie had failed one grade in the upper-elementary school but since that time had been advanced through the grades regularly with marks of D minus, despite the fact that by the time he arrived in high school he still could read only the simplest of the elementary-school books and had difficulty with arithmetic beyond multiplication of whole numbers.

A vocational interest inventory which all sophomores took upon entering high school showed that the boy's interests focused on things mechanical. After he had become sixteen years old in the middle of his year in ninth grade, his attendance at school had been increasingly sporadic, apparently because he now had a driver's license and was useful in his father's business.

In the face of this evidence, the teacher felt that the cause for Eddie's lack of adjustment to the American literature class was quite apparent: the boy could not read the material, nor did he care for the subject matter. Already as a high-school sophomore Eddie was finding a place in the adult world as a truck driver, a role which his family seemed to encourage. There appeared to be little reason for Eddie to be entranced by Robert Frost's *Mending Wall* or Poe's *Fall of the House of Usher*. The objectives of the school, as reflected by the required American literature, and the objectives of the boy and his family were quite at odds. Upon thinking over the matter, the teacher could no longer bring himself to blame a boy of low academic ability for not embracing schoolwork with enthusiasm.

Method of Treatment

The most appropriate move would have been to transfer Eddie to a different class, one which fitted its work to the needs and abilities of students of this type. But the high school was a small one, and no such class for slower learners existed. Therefore the teacher asked Eddie to stop after class. During the interview the instructor said he felt that their work in literature was not suiting Eddie's interests. The instructor would like to find some activities that would be more useful to Eddie. The boy appeared both surprised and suspicious. But when asked about his work with his father's trucking firm, he talked freely about where he drove and the problems he encountered on the job. When the teacher asked about the kinds of things a trucker had to read in his work, Eddie described the maps, the servicing manuals, and order forms that truckers used. He said that he also liked to look through magazines specializing in rebuilding antique cars and "customizing hot rods." The teacher suggested that he bring some of these magazines and manuals to school, and Eddie agreed.

During the ensuing weeks Eddie was excused from the usual literature homework. (He had never done it anyway, but he now received official sanction for his pattern of behavior, so he no longer needed to consider himself delinquent.) As substitute homework, he agreed to try assignments related to his trucking and automobile interests, such as answering questions from reading a road map, recognizing road signs, answering questions about reading that he had done in service manuals, preparing orders for parts from a mail-order catalogue, reading business letters, writing business letters, and the like. To better ensure that the assignments were done, the teacher kept them brief.

During class sessions Eddie was expected to listen to the regular discussion of literature and to the poems and stories that were read aloud. But the instructor agreed to mark him primarily on how well he completed his individualized assignments rather than on his success on the tests over literary works.

Success of Treatment

The treatment met with mixed success. Eddie now could be counted on to complete assignments more than half of the time. When he stopped after school two days a week to discuss what he was to do and how he had succeeded on the last assignment, he was serious and interested. He appeared to appreciate the interest his English teacher showed in him. He saw that he was learning things important in the work he did outside of school. But in class he continued to make smart-alec remarks that had a disrupting influence. The teacher estimated that he did this out of defense. The boy still felt inadequate to handle the intellectual concepts of American literature, so he tried to show disdain for them. His jibes, though still somewhat disturbing for the class, were now limited to remarks about classmates or authors being discussed, and were no longer directed at the teacher, even by implication.

By the end of the year the teacher concluded that his success with Eddie had been less than he had hoped but still worth the effort he had expended on the boy.

CASE V: AN ABSENCE OF READING SKILL

Three points are illustrated in the case of Parker Willis. First, students who are retarded educationally often will gain immediate, constant rewards for their efforts to progress if they are placed in competition with their own past performance rather than only with their more able age-mates. Second, a teacher may improve her estimate of a pupil's reading potential by testing the pupil's ability to learn aurally, that is, the ability to listen. Third, some students progress well in remedying their educational handicaps if they are in the classroom of a skillful instructor who combines a hard-boiled, unyielding approach toward classroom behavior with a warm-hearted concern for individual students and their problems.

The Problem Situation

Parker Willis was a shy, handsome Negro boy who, as an eighteen-year-old high-school junior, moved with his family from Southern California to a city in the middle of the state. When he enrolled in the high school in his new location, the program adviser suggested he enter an elective course in reading, because the boy's record of academic failure and his extremely low entrance-test scores indicated that reading disability was one of his major problems.

On his first day in the reading class, while the rest of the students worked silently in their individual books, the teacher asked him to sit with her in one corner of the room and read a passage aloud. She later described the performance in these terms:

He couldn't even pronounce words like "and." His reading was just a jumble of grunts. He had no idea about what he was doing. I had never seen a poorer performance in my forty years of teaching. Here he was, age eighteen and a nonreader.

An Estimate of Underlying Cause

Initially the teacher had no adequate clues to which of many possible causes were behind the boy's disability. She did not know whether his general intellectual ability was low, because the group tests of ability which he had taken had required him to read, so his failure on them might have been due to his reading disability rather than general intellectual shortcomings. She knew almost nothing about the quality of his past schooling, so she could not estimate whether his problem lay in faulty instruction in other schools. Thus, she adopted three methods of improving her estimate of the boy's potential:

First, she discussed with Parker his earlier experiences in school. He said that he originally was from the South, but that his family had moved a great deal. His earliest schools were apparently substandard institutions, and in recent years he was seldom in one school long enough to become well established socially or educationally. The teacher had already noticed that he was a "loner." He apparently had no friends at all in school. She also learned that he thought he would never be able to read. This appeared to disturb him greatly. She told him that she had never known a high-school boy who could not learn to read, and she was confident that he was no exception.

Second, after a month or so she asked Parker questions about information she had given to the class two and three weeks earlier. Her purpose was to learn whether he had understood and had remembered the oral portion of classwork. She learned that indeed he had. This helped confirm her growing impression that:

He wasn't a stupid boy. Like so many poor readers who are still basically bright enough, he had learned to be a good listener, because that was the way he could get along. The excellent readers often don't listen to me in class, because they know they can learn it by reading. But poor readers like Parker make the most of listening.

Third, she began giving him individual instruction. This enabled her to appraise carefully his rate of learning.

On the basis of these three sources of information, the teacher at the end of three months had developed a more optimistic view of Parker's potential than she had assumed when he had first entered class as a nonreader. She now believed that he was bright enough intellectually. His problem, as far as she could ascertain, had been caused primarily by his history of erratic schooling, oftentimes in substandard classrooms. Possibly he had also been a slow maturer in his early years, and emotional problems within the family might have contributed to his confusion in school and his marked shyness. In any event, she saw hope for him, particularly since he had become highly motivated to work at reading, now that he saw a chance that he finally could learn after so many years of failing.

Method of Treatment

A few remarks about the teacher's general operation of her five classes in reading (two classes for good readers who wanted additional improvement, three classes for retarded readers) will clarify the academic setting in which Parker confronted his reading problem.

One veteran of the class, in commenting on the teacher's operation of her classroom, said, "She sails a very tight ship. Nobody fools around in there."

At the beginning of the year the teacher announced to the class:

You have chosen this class so you can become a better reader. I'm sure that's what you will become, but it will mean hard work. To make this classroom a good place in which to read, we have some rules to follow.

The first has to do with who talks in class. If I want to say something to you, I shall ask for your attention and I shall say it. If you want to say something to me raise your hand and I'll give you an opportunity. But there is nothing you will need to say to your classmates. Your reading would be disturbed if students were allowed to talk to each other in this room, so there will be none of it.

Second, if you must move from place to place in the room, you will walk in a clockwise direction. This prevents the bumping and scuffling that could disturb your reading. People don't bump into each other when they are walking in the same direction.

Third, you see on the baseboard across the front of the room there are five chalk marks, one for each row of desks. You are to be sure that your row is lined up with the appropriate mark so that the aisles between desks are a proper width and no one will bump your desk and bother you.

Fourth, every minute that you are in this class is valuable. All of our time must be used for learning to read better. Each day we shall have one reading activity which the whole class completes together, but the rest of the time each person will work on his own assignment that I prepare for his own special needs. You will always know ahead of time what this assignment is, so you can work at it on your own. When you enter the room, begin with your special reading while I take roll and make out the absence slips. Every minute is valuable and will be used for reading.

In such a no-nonsense climate the reading activities were conducted. The success which the teacher achieved with her program was due primarily to four factors: (1) the teacher's making an individual diagnosis of each pupil's reading pattern so as to note both strengths and weaknesses, (2) the availability of a wide variety of reading materials from which to give assignments to suit individual problems, (3) a continual—almost daily—appraisal by the instructor of each student's progress, and (4) the teacher's constantly informing each student of his current strengths and shortcomings.

To accomplish the first of these steps—providing an initial diagnosis—the teacher assigned students to read a variety of kinds of materials in class the first week of school and to answer questions about what they had read. Most of the reading was silent, and most of the questions were mimeographed ones to be answered in written form. But each student also read one passage aloud to the teacher so she could learn which words he skipped or guessed or mispronounced.

A large store of different books and periodicals was in the permanent classroom collection. This supply was supplemented by books borrowed from the library on a one- or two-month loan and by current magazines which parents provided.

All students were required to respond to each reading assignment by answering one or more questions. In some cases everyone in class, or a cluster of students working on a particular skill, read the same material and answered the same questions, which were written for them on the blackboard or on a mimeographed sheet. However, quite often everyone did not face the same task. Instead, the teacher wrote individual assignments designed to aid a given student with the next step toward developing a needed skill. In other cases the teacher heard a student read aloud, and she gave an oral assignment to carry him beyond the stage which his oral reading showed he had reached.

To teach this way, the instructor had to spend many hours analyzing students' written responses and keeping records of their individual progress. She also had to display ingenuity in devising suitable questions for the students to answer. In regard to the questions, she said:

> I never like the questions the reading books suggest at the end of the chapter. They are too impersonal. I try to ask questions that relate to the student's own experiences, like: "How was the main character in this story of the West like Lucus Freeborn in the story of the *Dark Stranger,* which you read a couple of months ago?" Or: "If you were going to do what the author of this article did—that is, tell about quaint places in a city—what places would you describe in our own city, and why would you choose them?"

To keep students informed about their progress, she wrote comments on their papers, talked with them individually, and marked the papers with what she termed "old-fashioned percentages." She explained this system to the students in this manner:

The percentage shows what proportion of the assignment you did correctly. It tells about how well you understood this reading passage. I don't expect you to get 100 percent on your assignments. You are not in here to compete with anybody else in the class. You are only competing with yourself, and the percentage helps you see how you are getting along with this. So you are to compete with the percentage mark that you earned on your most recent paper. If you received 20 percent on that paper, you are to try to get a 22 or a 25 next time. If you can show such progress as this, that's just fine. If you got 5 percent last time, try to make it 10 percent next time. If you got 70 percent, let's see if you can reach 72 or 75 on the next assignment. You are here to become a better reader day after day. You are not here to compete with any of your classmates.

The foregoing pattern of teaching, then, represented this reading teacher's instructional style. This was the general pattern under which Parker Willis worked from the middle of his junior year through the end of his senior year in high school.

Just as the teacher designed some specific goals for each of the pupils, she had in mind the following ones for Parker. Since the boy was the most disabled reader in school, she decided that he would first need to begin with the most elementary phonics so that he could learn to pronounce the words he saw in print. He would also need a heavy fare of other word-attack skills: the use of prefixes and suffixes, the use of context, the use of a dictionary. He would need much praise for the small successes he might achieve, so that he could overcome the lack of self-confidence which had plagued his attempts to read so far in his school experiences. While learning these most basic reading skills, he would need to work along with his classmates to discover how to infer meanings which authors intend but do not explicitly state, to understand the use of figures of speech, and to compare what different authors have said about the same things. Parker would need to read as broadly as feasible in literature, science, history, the social sciences, and current events so as to succeed better in his other school subjects and become generally better informed about "what has been so far locked away from him in books."

The teacher began with the phonics instruction. Each day she spent fifteen minutes of the class period with him while the other students worked at individual reading assignments. Parker also came to her room during the teacher's free period, which was the boy's study-hall period, in order to secure further individual help or to pursue a silent reading task. This schedule continued for several months until the boy's progress permitted him to work more on his own without so much individualized attention. However, he still used many of his study-hall periods for additional reading instruction.

To work with Parker, the teacher developed a scheme for teaching phonics to older, disabled readers of his variety. In these first stages, he was required to read orally as often as possible—to sound out each word. He was not urged to speed up his reading, nor was he cautioned against moving his lips when he read silently. The teacher held a strong conviction that:

> So much emphasis is put on reading fast that many students try to speed over the material rather than to catch all of the meaning. My trouble usually is to convince them to slow down so they get the ideas clearly in mind and not to hurry by.

Parker's initial progress was very slow; but gradually he began to master phonics, and his reading vocabulary increased. With this improvement, he felt encouraged, so his level of motivation increased. By the middle of the following year he had sufficiently conquered his shyness and had improved his oral reading so that he was prepared to accept a special challenge. The teacher gave him an article from *The New York Times* which he was to practice at home in preparation for reading it aloud to the class. On the day he performed, his classmates were assigned to listen carefully and summarize the contents of the article and give it an appropriate title. Parker's reading was so accurate and clear that the other students had no difficulty in fulfilling their assignment.

Success of Treatment

Near the end of his senior year, Parker admitted to the teacher that "I've been afraid for a long time that when I had a family of my own, my children would be ashamed of a papa who couldn't read. I don't want to shame them."

The teacher said, "Anybody who can read to an audience the way you did the other day is somebody to be proud of. If your children ever want to know how well you read, have them ask me."

The remarkable success the boy had achieved during the year and a half in the reading class was shown on the final standardized testing which came at the close of the senior year. Whereas in his junior year he had hardly been able to make out any words, at the end of his senior year he read as well as an average tenth grader. If he had not been basically an intellectually able boy, he could not have made such progress. As his teacher had surmised earlier, Parker apparently had suffered from a history of inadequate teaching, sporadic schooling, and perhaps developmental immaturity at the time of his earliest reading experiences. Such a history could understandably lead to discouragement and a low assessment of his own abilities, so that a resulting set of negative emotions would develop to make the reading problem even more difficult to correct. But the high-school reading teacher's businesslike classroom organization, her individual attention, and the boy's own determination to master reading enabled him finally to succeed.

By the time of graduation, Parker was still a shy boy with few friends. However, he obviously was more confident in both social and academic situations than he had been a year earlier. His teacher and his counselor attributed these social and academic gains primarily to the boy's growth in reading. He had proved to himself that he could achieve what he had earlier feared was an impossible goal.

CASE VI: ACADEMIC RETARDATION AND HYPOCHONDRIA

The case of Claire Lasalle shows how a teacher of the educationally handicapped used programed materials as a means of suiting instruction to the individual learning patterns of her students.

The Problem Situation

A portion of a faculty meeting in a large suburban high school was set aside for the teacher of a new supplementary class for educationally handicapped students to describe the nature of her work. As she told the staff, her work was with only ten or twelve students, each of whom attended regular classes in the school most of the day, but who met with her for several hours a week for special help. To qualify for her class, they had to show learning difficulties associated with emotional or neurological disorders, but they were not to be physically handicapped or mentally retarded. In other words, her students were sound of body and were at least average in general intelligence, yet they succeeded badly in school.

After she had finished describing her methods of working with these disturbed pupils, another member of the faculty asked her privately, "How does one go about enrolling a student in your class? My niece, who is a junior in school here, needs your help." When the record of the niece was investigated, it was clear that she did indeed qualify. Thus, early in the spring of her junior year, Claire Lasalle entered the special class.

The girl's problems were several. She was a poor reader, a worse writer, and a somewhat inadequate speaker. Since she was thus disabled in fundamental communication skills, her work in most academic areas was of failing quality.

Claire had been nicknamed "Crampy" by her schoolmates, because she frequently complained of cramps and was permitted to leave school and go home to bed. She also complained of other vague maladies, like headaches and weakness. Her parents, greatly concerned over the girl's health, did everything possible to make life comfortable when she was home ill.

The girl's inordinate concern with health also manifested itself in a marked fear of germs and of moisture that might be in the classroom or on the desk when she entered class.

Despite her cramps and headaches, the physician who gave her a physical examination pronounced her basically in sound health. The psychologist who examined her said that she was of at least average ability. In short, she easily qualified for the special class.

An Estimate of Underlying Cause

During the early weeks that Claire was in her class, the teacher tried to learn the nature and causes of the girl's problem through talking with her, observing the way she succeeded with school tasks, talking with her parents, and making informal evaluations of her communication skills.

From the girl's health records the teacher learned that Claire had been an average student until seventh grade, when she was injured in an auto accident and spent several weeks at home recuperating. Since that time her grades had been poor, and her attendance had been erratic.

The teacher's observations of Claire's learning habits suggested that the girl may have suffered brain damage in the auto accident. For example, when Claire learned facts for her history or English lessons, the facts quickly slipped out of mind. One of her greatest problems was remembering the meanings of words. She had trouble handling any concepts beyond the simplest and most obvious. For instance, she could never see the connection between motive and action in a story. She could not contrast or compare two objects or ideas.

Reading was so distasteful to the girl that she refused even to attempt a reading test. However, the teacher, by gradually developing a bond of friendship with Claire, managed to entice her into trying passages from popular magazines and books that represented several levels of difficulty. On the basis of her performance, the teacher judged that she had the reading skill of the average sixth grader. Her writing skills were those of a fourth grader, her speech that of a seventh grader.

The teacher did not depend solely on her own judgment for diagnosing Claire's problems. She also conferred periodically with the school system's psychiatrist to secure guidance in her work with Claire and with her other educationally handicapped students.

By the end of the spring semester, after Claire had been receiving special help three times a week for several months, the remedial teacher concluded that the girl suffered some aphasia, that is, her power to understand speech was impaired. Claire also appeared to be a hypochondriac. The hypochondria may well have begun at the time of the auto accident when her parents had lavished love and care on her. The teacher guessed that in subsequent years as Claire faced difficult problems and yearned for escape, an imagined or psychogenic attack of cramps or a headache enabled her to retreat to her bed where she was consoled by her parents' loving care.

Methods of Treatment

The first months of Claire's remedial sessions were dedicated mostly to the teacher's gaining the girl's confidence and furnishing some aid with reading and providing exercises for neuro-motor training. However, as the teacher stated in her June report, "Claire's frequent absences greatly reduced her sessions with the remedial specialist. Her progress has been insufficient to warrant a full report at this time. She should be retained in the educationally handicapped program next year."

The following September the teacher adopted an unyielding attitude toward the girl's apparent hypochondria. She told Claire's parents that they had babied her too much and that if they wanted the girl to succeed, they would have to insist that she not escape problems through becoming ill. The teacher told Claire, "This year you're not staying home in bed. If you fail to appear for one of our sessions, I'm coming home to get you."

The first time Claire was absent in the fall, the teacher telephoned the home and reminded the girl's mother that the doctor had said Claire's health was satisfactory. She added, "If Claire doesn't get over here today, I'm through trying to help her." In a short time the girl arrived. After two similar incidents, her attendance improved dramatically and she began to progress.

Now that Claire came to school regularly, it was the teacher's task to discover how the girl could be motivated to improve her communication skills rather than to continue avoiding them. The teacher later explained her approach in this manner:

With each of my educationally handicapped students I start with whatever is healthy and positive about him and build a

program of study around this. From observing Claire and talking with her, I found she had a great interest in people and
in social activities, so I started her on an individualized psychology course. This deeply interested her, and we were on
our way.

Several of the other educationally handicapped students, also
interested in psychology, joined Claire in her study. A developmental reading program to improve the students' vocabularies
and comprehension was coupled with their work on child psychology and the nature of the nervous system. Claire was also
given training in perception.

To help reduce the emotional blocks which Claire and several
classmates had developed toward reading and writing, her teacher
continually pointed out that "What you think, you can say; what
you can say, you can write; what you can write, you can read."
As the students became engrossed in their discussions of the psychological factors that affected their lives, the teacher had them
write down what they were saying. Later, when they looked at
what they had written, they found reading their own ideas to be
a simple task which they performed unafraid.

In addition to preparing her own learning materials, the
teacher drew heavily on the programed textbooks and simple
teaching machines which have been developed in recent years.
For example, during the latter part of Claire's senior year she
and several classmates worked—each at his own speed—in Daniel
P. Kimble's *Physiological Psychology* (Addison-Wesley Publish-
ing Co., 1966). This proved to be a demanding task, for the
vocabulary was not easy. However, the students found it satisfying because after reading each two or three sentences, they were
required to fill in a word in the next sentence to demonstrate
how well they had understood the material; and they immediately
learned the correctness of their answer by looking at the correct
response printed in the margin.

Throughout the year the students also used programed materials that aided them with the work of their regular high-school
classes. A disk-shaped teaching machine helped them master historical facts. In addition, they wrote their own questions about

historical events to ask each other, and Claire used flash cards about historical characters to "over-learn" historical facts which in the past had readily slipped out of mind. To supplement the study of composition which was part of her work in psychology, she used the programed English text *English 3200* (Harcourt, Brace & World, Inc.) for improving her understanding of usage. In her final semester, Claire's remedial teacher cooperated with the business-education instructor in providing the girl with a programed correspondence course on business practice.

The two major projects that demanded the attention of the educationally handicapped students near the close of the year were the presentation of a panel discussion about psychology and the development of materials for a motion picture.

In preparation for the discussion, the students invited several high-school administrators and directors of the city's special-education department. The less-able students were given simpler responsibilities like greeting the guests and serving refreshments. Claire, however, was now one of the best readers and speakers, so she was a member of the panel. When her turn came, she presented her ideas clearly from well-written notes. Her teacher, in commenting on the girl's performance, said:

> Claire was reading eleventh- and twelfth-grade vocabulary. But since she was doing her reading from notes about physiological psychology which she had prepared, she didn't realize the level of difficulty of the terms and so was not intimidated by them. When she had first entered the remedial class last year she had shown great difficulty remembering English and history facts from one day to the next. However, psychological terms had come to mean something personal to her, for they explained some things about the way she and others behaved. These terms she could remember.

The filming of a motion picture served to culminate a project that the students in the remedial group had pursued through the final months of the school year. The project had started with a discussion about a shaggy dog the teacher owned. She had brought the dog to class and had posed several questions about his actions in order to stimulate the class members to think about his behavior and pattern of learning. As a next step in their study of comparative psychology, the students observed children at a nearby nursery school. They discussed the ways children learn, and each student wrote a short story for children with the shaggy dog serving as the central character. Some students drew illustrations for their stories. Claire's story was one of the best. The remedial-class students also speculated about effective ways to teach small children. To test their ideas, they planned games to teach to preschool groups and tried out the games at the nursery school.

Throughout the shaggy-dog unit the high-school pupils were enthusiastic about their work. Reading, writing, and speaking experiences grew naturally out of their studies of animal and human behavior.

At the end of the semester the teacher suggested that they produce a colored motion picture tracing their shaggy-dog activities. A local school of photography provided the equipment and cameramen. The high-school's art department prepared the film titles. The remedial teacher, in discussions with her students, directed the preparation of a script. And finally, each of the educationally handicapped students was given a role to play in the film to demonstrate the steps they had taken in their project. However, this plan to have each student recorded on film was not a complete success. Two of the students disappeared on the day they were to appear before the camera. One left school entirely, and the other was found smoking in a remote area of the campus. Commenting on this development, the teacher said:

> It shows I had pushed them too fast. I had thought they all had grown enough in self-esteem to play a part in the film. But the ones who ran away apparently could not yet bear to see themselves as they really were. In their minds I think they held a pleasant, complimentary, but tenuous image of themselves. They seemed to fear that the camera would show the image was but a dream.

But Claire was different. On the appointed day, she appeared on time, well groomed, suitably dressed, and eager to play her part. She played it well.

Success of Treatment

The success of the teacher's efforts was shown in Claire's improved school attendance, her higher marks in regular high-school classes, and her growth in responsibility and leadership. Interlaced with these improvements was an overall increase in self-confidence.

During Claire's year and four months in the remedial group, her attendance pattern changed from one of frequent absences to one of almost perfect attendance. This improvement was apparently the result of: (1) the teacher's pursuing Claire when she stayed home and insisting that the girl show up at school immediately and (2) Claire's growing satisfaction with her success in studying psychology, reading, and writing. Her progress was bringing her welcome praise from her teachers, particularly from the instructor of the remedial group.

In regard to school marks Claire also achieved significant growth. In the spring of her junior year she had been failing in all subjects. At the end of her senior year she earned B's and C's in all classes except history, in which she received a D. Her remedial teacher, commenting on the mark in history, said:

> Claire simply did not have enough time to catch up. For years she had been missing historical facts and the relationships among historical events. It was too late in her senior year to build up the memory bank that her classmates had developed throughout their junior- and senior-high-school years. But the fact that in her senior year her scores on history tests jumped from 30's and 40's into the 70's shows the progress she was making by the time of graduation. If she had had more time and more over-learning of historical materials, she would have been able to achieve as well in this subject as she had in her others.

As Claire's skills improved, she grew noticeably in self-regard, a fact which manifested itself in the leadership she began to exert within the remedial group. She took responsibility for aiding less able classmates, for directing group activities, and for keeping the class working when the teacher had to be out of the room.

At the time of graduation, her remedial teacher concluded:

Her greatest growth has been in self-esteem. She has proved to herself that she is a very satisfactory young lady, quite capable of succeeding with both intellectual and social tasks. A year ago she and her parents had feared she would never graduate. Now she has graduated with quite a respectable senior-year record. She well deserves her self-esteem.

INDEX

181